LIFE

FAITH

LIFE

FAITH

The Portable New Century Edition

EMANUEL SWEDENBORG

Translated from the Latin by George F. Dole

SWEDENBORG FOUNDATION
West Chester, Pennsylvania

Originally published in Latin (Amsterdam, 1763) as two separate works:
 Doctrina Vitae pro Nova Hierosolyma ex Praeceptis Decalogi
 Doctrina Novae Hierosolymae de Fide

Printed in the United States of America

ISBN   978-0-87785-413-5
This text is also included in the hardcover library edition of *The Shorter Works of 1763*, ISBN 978-0-87785-503-3.

Library of Congress Cataloging-in-Publication Data

Swedenborg, Emanuel, 1688-1772, author.
   [Works. Selections. English]
   Life/faith / Emanuel Swedenborg ; translated by George F. Dole.
      pages cm
   Summary: "Two short works, which Emanuel Swedenborg originally published separately, containing his teachings on religious faith and its connection with the way one lives. In "Life," Swedenborg focuses on regeneration (the conscious process of spiritual rebirth) and interprets the Ten Commandments in light of people's choices between good and evil. In "Faith," he rejects the notion of faith without rational sense, and he emphasizes that true faith can occur only in tandem with love and kindness for others"-- Provided by publisher.
      ISBN 978-0-87785-413-5 (paperback)
      1. New Jerusalem Church--Doctrines. I. Dole, George F., translator. II. Swedenborg, Emanuel, 1688-1772. Doctrina vitae pro Nova Hierosolyma ex praeceptis decalogi. English. III. Swedenborg, Emanuel, 1688-1772. Doctrina Novae Hierosolymae de fide. English. IV. Title.

BX8712.D96 2014

289'.4--DC23

                                                                          2014042278

Senior copy editor, Alicia L. Dole
Text designed by Joanna V. Hill
Ornaments from the first Latin edition, 1763
Typesetting by Alicia L. Dole
Cover designed by Karen Connor

For information contact:
Swedenborg Foundation
320 North Church Street
West Chester, PA 19380 USA
Telephone: (610) 430-3222
Web: www.swedenborg.com
E-mail: info@swedenborg.com

Conventions Used in This Work

Most of the following conventions apply generally to the translations in the New Century Edition Portable series. For introductory material on the content and history of *Life* and *Faith,* and for annotations on their subject matter, with an extensive index, the reader is referred to the Deluxe New Century Edition volume *The Shorter Works of 1763.*

Section numbers Following a practice common in his time, Swedenborg divided his published theological works into sections numbered in sequence from beginning to end. His original section numbers have been preserved in this edition; they appear in boxes in the outside margins. Traditionally, these sections have been referred to as "numbers" and designated by the abbreviation "n." In this edition, however, the more common section symbol (§) is used to designate the section numbers, and the sections are referred to as such.

Subsection numbers Because many sections throughout Swedenborg's works are too long for precise cross-referencing, Swedenborgian scholar John Faulkner Potts (1838–1923) further divided them into subsections; these have since become standard, though minor variations occur from one edition to another. These subsections are indicated by bracketed numbers that appear in the text itself: [2], [3], and so on. Because the beginning of the first *subsection* always coincides with the beginning of the *section* proper, it is not labeled in the text.

Citations of Swedenborg's text As is common in Swedenborgian studies, text citations of Swedenborg's works refer not to page numbers but to section numbers, which are uniform in most editions. In citations the section symbol (§) is generally omitted after the title of a work by Swedenborg. Thus "*Heaven and Hell* 239" would refer to section 239 (§239) of Swedenborg's *Heaven and Hell,* not to page 239 of any edition. Subsection numbers are given after a colon; a reference such as "239:2" indicates subsection 2 of section 239. The reference "239:1" would indicate the first subsection of section 239, though that subsection is not in fact labeled in the text. Where section numbers stand alone without titles, their function is indicated by the prefixed section symbol; for example, "§239:2".

Citations of the Bible Biblical citations in this edition follow the accepted standard: a semicolon is used between book references and between chapter references, and a comma between verse references. Therefore "Matthew 5:11, 12; 6:1; 10:41, 42; Luke 6:23, 35" refers to Matthew chapter 5, verses 11 and 12; Matthew chapter 6, verse 1; Matthew chapter 10, verses 41 and 42; and Luke chapter 6, verses 23 and 35. Swedenborg often incorporated the numbers of verses not actually represented in his text when listing verse numbers for a passage he quoted; these apparently constitute a kind of "see also" reference to other material he felt was relevant, and are generally retained in this edition without annotation. This edition also follows Swedenborg where he cites contiguous verses individually (for example, John 14:8, 9, 10, 11), rather than as a range (John 14:8–11). Occasionally this edition supplies a full, conventional Bible reference where Swedenborg omits one after a quotation.

Quotations in Swedenborg Some features of the original Latin texts have been modernized in this edition. For example, Swedenborg's first editions rely on context or italics rather than on quotation marks to indicate passages taken from the Bible or from other works. The manner in which these conventions are used in the original suggests that Swedenborg did not feel it necessary to belabor the distinction between direct quotation and paraphrase; neither did he mark his omissions from or changes to material he quoted, a practice in which this edition generally follows him. One exception consists of those instances in which Swedenborg did not include a complete sentence at the beginning or end of a Bible quotation. The omission in such cases has been marked in this edition with added points of ellipsis.

Italicized terms Any words in indented scriptural extracts that are here set in italics reflect a similar emphasis in the first editions.

Swedenborg's footnote The author's footnote to *Life* 101, indicated by a superscript letter *a* in the main body of the text, includes cross-references to two of his previously published works.

Changes to and insertions in the text This translation is based on the first Latin editions, published by Swedenborg himself. It incorporates the silent emendation of minor errors, not only in the text proper but in Bible verse references and in section references to Swedenborg's other published theological works. The text has also been changed without notice where the verse numbering of the Latin Bible cited by Swedenborg differs from that of modern English Bibles. Throughout the translation, references or cross-references that are implied but not stated have been inserted in square brackets []; for example, [Matthew 22:40].

Biblical titles Swedenborg refers to the Hebrew Scriptures as the Old Testament and to the Greek Scriptures as the New Testament; his terminology has been adopted in this edition.

Teachings
about
Life
for the
New Jerusalem
Drawn from
the Ten Commandments

Teachings about Life for the New Jerusalem

Religion Is All about How We Live, and the Religious Way to Live Is to Do Good

EVERYONE who has any religion knows and acknowledges that people who lead a good life are saved and people who lead an evil life are damned. That is, they know and acknowledge that if we lead a good life we think good things not only about God but also about our neighbor, which is not the case if we lead an evil life.

What we love constitutes our life, and whatever we love we not only do freely but also think freely. So we say that life is doing good things because doing good things is inseparable from thinking good things. If this doing and this thinking are not working together in us, then they are not part of our life. This, though, needs to be explained in what follows.

As for the fact that religion is about how we live and that the [religious] way to live is to do good, everyone who reads the Word sees this and acknowledges it on reading it. We find the following in the Word:

> Whoever breaks the least of these commandments and teaches others to do the same will be called the least in the kingdom of the heavens, but whoever *does and teaches* [these commandments] will be called great in

3

the kingdom of the heavens. I tell you, unless your *righteousness* exceeds that of the scribes and Pharisees, you will not enter the kingdom of the heavens. (Matthew 5:19, 20)

Every tree that does not *bear good fruit* is cut down and thrown into the fire; therefore *by their fruits* you will know them. (Matthew 7:19, 20)

Not everyone who says to me, "Lord, Lord," will enter the kingdom of the heavens, but *those who do the will* of my Father who is in the heavens. (Matthew 7:21)

On that day many will say to me, "Lord, Lord, haven't we prophesied in your name and done many great things in your name?" But then I will declare to them, "I do not know you. Depart from me, *you workers of iniquity.*" (Matthew 7:22, 23)

Everyone who hears my words and *does them* I will liken to a wise man who built his house on the rock; but everyone who hears my words and *does not do them* will be likened to a foolish man who built his house on the sand. (Matthew 7:24, 26)

Jesus said, "A sower went out to sow. Some seed fell on a hard-packed path, some on stony ground, some among thorns, and some into good ground. The people who received seed in good ground are those who hear and understand the Word, and as a result *bear fruit and become productive,* some a hundredfold, some sixtyfold, and some thirtyfold." When he had said these things, Jesus cried out and said, "Those who have ears to hear must hear this." (Matthew 13:3–9, 23)

The Son of Humanity is going to come in the glory of his Father, and then *he will repay all people according to their deeds.* (Matthew 16:27)

The kingdom of God will be taken from you and given to *a nation that bears its fruits.* (Matthew 21:43)

When the Son of Humanity comes in his glory, then he will sit on the throne of his glory and will say to the sheep on his right, "Come, you who are blessed, and possess as your inheritance the kingdom prepared for you since the founding of the world; *because I was hungry and you gave me something to eat. I was thirsty and you gave me something to drink. I was a stranger and you took me in. I was naked and you clothed me. I was sick and you visited me. I was in prison and you came to me.*" Then the righteous will answer him, "When did we see you like this?" But the king will answer and say, "I tell you truly, as much as you did this to one of the least of my people, you did it to me." And the king will say similar things to the goats on the left, but since they had not done things like these, he will say, "Depart from me, you who are cursed, into the ever-lasting fire prepared for the Devil and his angels." (Matthew 25:31–46)

Bear fruit that is consistent with repentance. The axe is already lying against the root of the trees. Every tree *that does not bear good fruit* is cut down and thrown into the fire. (Luke 3:8, 9)

Jesus said, "Why do you call me 'Lord, Lord,' and *not do what I say?* Everyone who comes to me and hears what I am saying and *does it* is like someone building a house who laid its foundation on the rock; but anyone who hears and does nothing is like someone building a house on the ground without a foundation." (Luke 6:46–49)

Jesus said, "My mother and my brothers are these who hear the Word of God and *do it.*" (Luke 8:21)

Then you begin to stand outside and knock on the door, saying, "Lord, open the door for us!" But he will say in reply, "I do not know where you are from. *Depart from me, all you workers of iniquity.*" (Luke 13:25–27)

This is the condemnation, that light has come into the world, but peo-ple loved darkness rather than light, because *their deeds were evil.* All *who do evil* hate the light, because *their deeds* would be exposed; but those who do the truth come to the light so that *their deeds* may be clearly seen, because *their deeds were done in God.* (John 3:19–21)

Those who have done what is good will go forth into [the resurrection of life, but *those who have done what is evil* will go forth into] the resurrec-tion of condemnation. (John 5:29)

We know that God does not hear sinners; but he does hear people who worship God and *do his will.* (John 9:31)

If you know these things, *you are blessed if you do them.* (John 13:17)

The people who love me are those who have my commandments and *do them;* and I will love them and will manifest myself to them. I will come to them and make a home with them. Those who do not love me *do not keep my words.* (John 14:15, 21–24)

Jesus said, "I am the vine, and my Father is the vinedresser. Every branch in me *that does not bear fruit* he takes away; and every branch *that bears fruit* he prunes, so that *it will bear more fruit.*" (John 15:1, 2)

My Father is glorified *by your bearing much fruit* and becoming my disciples. (John 15:8)

You are my friends if you do whatever I command you. I have chosen you *so that you will bear fruit* and *your fruit will remain.* (John 15:14, 16)

The Lord said to John, "To the angel of the church of Ephesus write, '*I know your works.* I have this against you, that you have left your first *love.* Repent and *do the first works,* or else I will remove your lampstand from its place.'" (Revelation 2:1, 2, 4, 5)

To the angel of the church in Smyrna write, "*I know your works.*" (Revelation 2:8, 9)

To the angel of the church in Pergamum write, "*I know your works. Repent!*" (Revelation 2:12, 13, 16)

To the angel of the church in Thyatira write, "*I know your works and your love; your* last *works* are more than the first." (Revelation 2:18, 19)

To the angel of the church in Sardis write, "*I know your works,* that you have a name that you are alive, but you are dead. *I have not found your works perfect before God. Repent!*" (Revelation 3:1, 2, 3)

To the angel of the church in Philadelphia write, "*I know your works.*" (Revelation 3:7, 8)

To the angel of the church in Laodicea write, "*I know your works. Repent!*" (Revelation 3:14, 15, 19)

I heard a voice from heaven saying, "Write: 'Blessed are the dead who die in the Lord from now on.'" "[Yes,]" says the spirit, "so that they may rest from their labors, and *their works follow them.*" (Revelation 14:13)

A book was opened, which is the Book of Life. And the dead were judged by the things that were written in the book; *all* were judged *according to their works.* (Revelation 20:12, 13)

Behold, I am coming quickly, and my reward is with me, *to give to all according to what they have done.* (Revelation 22:12)

In the Old Testament, too:

Repay them *according to their work and according to the deeds of their hands.* (Jeremiah 25:14)

Jehovah, whose eyes are open to all the ways of humankind, *to give to all according to their ways and according to the fruit of their deeds* . . . (Jeremiah 32:19)

I will punish them *according to their ways* and repay them *according to their deeds.* (Hosea 4:9)

Jehovah deals with us *according to our ways* and *according to our deeds.* (Zechariah 1:6)

There are also many passages where it says that we are to *do* the statutes, commandments, and laws, such as the following:

Keep my statutes and my judgments. *Anyone who does so will live by means of them.* (Leviticus 18:5)

You shall observe all my statutes and my judgments *by doing them.* (Leviticus 19:37; 20:8; 22:31)

The children of Israel were promised blessings *if they did the precepts* and curses *if they did not do them* (Leviticus 26:3–46). They were commanded to make for themselves a fringe on the hems of their garments to remind them of all the precepts of Jehovah *so that they would do them* (Numbers 15:38, 39)—and there are thousands more passages.

Then too, the Lord teaches in parables that works are what make us part of the church and that our salvation depends on them. Many of his parables are about those who do good being accepted and those who do evil being rejected. See, for example, the parable of the workers in the vineyard (Matthew 21:33–44), the parable of the fig tree that bore no fruit (Luke 13:6 and following), the parable of the talents and the minas which those [in the parable] were to use in business (Matthew 25:14–31; Luke 19:12–25), the parable of the Samaritan who bound up the wounds of the man beaten by robbers (Luke 10:30–37), the parable of the rich man and Lazarus (Luke 16:19–31), and the parable of the ten young women (Matthew 25:1–12).

Everyone who has any religion knows and acknowledges that those **3** who lead a good life are saved and those who lead an evil life are damned. They know this because heaven is united with people who know from the Word that there is a God, that there is a heaven and a hell, and that there is a life after death. This [connection with heaven] gives rise to this widespread perception.

For this reason in the Athanasian statement of faith concerning the Trinity, which is accepted throughout the whole Christian world, what it says at the end is also accepted everywhere, namely,

> Jesus Christ, who suffered for our salvation, ascended into heaven, and sits at the right hand of the Father Almighty. From there he will come to judge the living and the dead; and *then those who have done good will go into everlasting life and those who have done evil will go into everlasting fire.*

4 Even so, there are many people in Christian churches who teach that it is faith alone that saves, and living a good life or doing what is good has nothing to do with it. They even go so far as to teach that living an evil life or doing what is evil does not damn those who have been justified by faith alone, because they are in God and in grace. Strange as it may seem, though, despite the fact that this is what they teach, they still have an acknowledgment (which comes from that widespread perception bestowed by heaven) that people are saved if they live a good life and damned if they live an evil life. We can see this acknowledgment in the *prayer* that is read to people who are taking the Holy Supper in churches in Britain and in Germany, Sweden, and Denmark. It is common knowledge that there are people in these countries who teach faith alone. The prayer that is read in Britain to people taking the sacrament of the Supper is the following.

5 & 6 The way and means to be received as worthy partakers of that Holy Table [the Holy Supper] is, first, to examine your lives and conversations [dealings with others] by the rule of God's commandments, and wherever you shall perceive yourselves to have offended either by will, word, or deed, there to bewail your own sinfulness, and to confess yourselves to Almighty God, with full purpose of amendment of life; and if you shall perceive your offences to be such as are not only against God, but also against your neighbors, then you shall reconcile yourselves to them, being ready to make restitution and satisfaction according to the utmost of your power, for all injuries and wrongs done by you to any other, and being likewise ready to forgive others that have offended you, as you would have forgiveness of your offences from God's hand; for otherwise the receiving of the Holy Communion does nothing else but increase your damnation. Therefore if any of you be a blasphemer of God, or a hinderer or slanderer of his Word, or an adulterer, or be in malice or envy or in any other grievous crime, repent of your sins, or else do not come to the Holy Table; lest after the taking of that Holy Sacrament the Devil enter into you, as he entered into

Judas, and fill you full of all iniquities, and bring you to destruction of both body and soul.

I was granted the opportunity in the spiritual world to question some **7** elders from Britain who believed in and preached faith alone. I asked them whether when they were in church and read this prayer—which does not mention faith—they really believed that if people did evil things and did not repent, the Devil would enter into them as he had into Judas and would destroy both body and soul. They said that when they were in the state they were in when they read the prayer, they simply knew and thought that this was the essence of their religion, but when they were composing and polishing their own speeches or sermons they did not think along the same lines. This was because they were focusing on faith as the sole means of salvation and of living a good life as a moral side effect useful for the public welfare.

All the same, they held the conviction, which was also a matter of common sense for them, that people who live a good life are saved and that people who live an evil life are damned; and they felt this way whenever they were not wrapped up in themselves.

The reason religion is all about how we live is that after death we all **8** are our own life. It remains the same for us as it was in the world and does not change. An evil life cannot be altered into a good one or a good life into an evil one, because they are opposites, and alteration into something opposite is extinction. So because they are opposites, a good life is called life and an evil life is called death.

That is why religion is all about how we live and why the way to live is to do good. On our nature after death being determined by our life in the world see *Heaven and Hell* 470–484.

No One Can Do Anything Genuinely Good
on His or Her Own

THE reason hardly any of us has known whether our good actions **9** were coming from ourselves or from God is that the church has divorced faith from caring, and doing good comes from caring. We give to the poor; help those in need; endow churches and hostels; are considerate of our church, our country, and our fellow citizens; attend church regularly and worship and pray devoutly when we do; read the Word and religious literature; and think about our salvation—all without knowing whether our actions come from ourselves or from God. These same actions can come from ourselves or from God. If these actions come from God, they are good; if they come from ourselves, they are not good. In fact, there are acts that in and of themselves resemble good ones and yet are obviously evil—hypocritical good deeds, for example, that are deceptive and deliberately misleading.

10 Good deeds that come from God and good deeds that come from ourselves could be compared to gold. Gold that is nothing but gold and is called unalloyed gold is good gold. Gold that is alloyed with silver is gold, too, but its value depends on the alloy, while gold alloyed with copper is less valuable.

Artificial gold, though, and things given the color of gold, are not good; there is no real gold in them.

There is also gilding. There is gilt silver, copper, iron, tin, and lead, and also gilt wood and gilt stone. They may look like gold superficially, but since they are not gold they are valued according to their artistry or the cost of the gilding or the cost of the gold that can be stripped from them. This value is as different from that of gold as the value of clothes is from the value of the one who is wearing them.

For that matter, you can cover rotten wood or slag or even excrement with gold. This is "gold" that could be compared to pharisaical "good works."

11 We can tell by science whether gold is substantially good, whether it is alloyed or fake, or whether it is just gilding; but science cannot tell us whether the good we are doing is essentially good. All we know is that good actions that come from God are good and good actions that come from ourselves are not good; so since it is important for our salvation to know whether the good things we are doing come from God or not, this needs to be revealed. Before it is revealed, though, something needs to be said about good works.

12 There are good works that are civic, good works that are moral, and good works that are spiritual. Good works that are civic are things we do because of civic law. To the extent that we practice civic goodness, we are citizens of this earthly world. Good works that are moral are things we do because of rational law. To the extent that we practice moral goodness, we are human. Good works that are spiritual are things we do because of spiritual law. To the extent that we practice spiritual goodness, we are citizens of the spiritual world.

These types of goodness follow in this sequence: spiritual goodness is highest, moral goodness is intermediate, and civic goodness is lowest.

If we have spiritual goodness we are moral and civic individuals as well; but if we do not have spiritual goodness we may seem to be moral and civic individuals but in fact we are not.

The reason we are moral and civic if we have spiritual goodness is that spiritual goodness contains within itself the essence of what is good and is the source of moral and civic goodness. The only possible source of the real essence of goodness is the one who is goodness itself. Cast the net of your thinking as wide as you will, concentrate, and ask what makes good good, and you will see that it is its essence; a good deed is good if it has the essence of goodness within it. This means that a deed is good if it originates in goodness itself—in God. So if some good deed originates not in God but in ourselves, it is not good.

You can see from what it says in §§27, 28, and 38 of *Teachings on Sacred Scripture* that what is first, what is intermediate, and what is last make a single entity like a purpose, a means, and a result; and because they do make a single entity, the purpose itself is called the primary purpose, the means is an intermediate purpose, and the result is the final purpose. So you must see that for us, if we have spiritual goodness, our moral goodness is spiritual on the intermediate level, and our civic goodness is spiritual on the lowest level.

That is why, as already noted, if we have spiritual goodness we are moral and civic individuals as well; but if we do not have spiritual goodness we are neither moral nor civic but only seem to be. We seem to be to ourselves and to others as well.

The reason we can still think and therefore talk rationally, like spiritual people, even when we ourselves are not spiritual is that our understanding can be raised into heaven's light, which is truth, and can see things on that basis. However, our will cannot in the same way be lifted into heaven's warmth, which is love, and act on that basis.

That is why truth and love are not united in us unless we are spiritual. It is also why we possess the power of speech. This actually is what differentiates us from animals. It is because our understanding can be raised into heaven when our will has not yet been raised that we can be reformed and can become spiritual. We are not reformed and do not become spiritual, though, until our will has been raised.

Because at first our understanding has more of this ability than our will does, we are able to think and therefore talk rationally like spiritual people no matter what our nature, even if we are evil. However, the reason we are not rational is that our understanding does not lead our will. Rather, our will leads our understanding, as noted in §115 of *Teachings on Sacred Scripture.* All understanding does is teach us and show us the way; and as long as our will is not one with our understanding in heaven, we are not spiritual and therefore are not rational. You see, when we are left to our will or love, then we toss out our rational thinking about God, heaven, and eternal life and instead pick up whatever agrees with our will or love and call this "rational." But this will be given further attention in the works on angelic wisdom.

16   In what follows, people who do good actions that come from themselves will be called "earthly people," since their moral and civic behavior is earthly in essence; while people who do good actions that come from the Lord will be called "spiritual people," because their moral and civic behavior is spiritual in essence.

17   The Lord tells us in John that no one can do anything that is genuinely good on his or her own:

> People cannot receive anything unless it has been given to them from heaven. (John 3:27)

And again,

> Those who abide in me and in whom I abide bear much fruit, because without me you cannot do anything. (John 15:5)

"Those who abide in me and in whom I abide bear much fruit" means that everything good comes from the Lord—"fruit" meaning what is good. "Without me you cannot do anything" means that none of us can do good on our own.

People who believe in the Lord and who do what is good from him are called "children of the light" (John 12:36; Luke 16:8), "children of the wedding" (Mark 2:19), "children of the resurrection" (Luke 20:36), "children of God" (Luke 20:36; John 1:12), and those "born of God"

(John 1:13). It says that "they will see God" (Matthew 5:8), that "the Lord will make a home with them" (John 14:23), that they "have the faith of God" (Mark 11:22), and that "their deeds have been done in God" (John 3:21).

These statements are summed up in the following words:

> As many as received Jesus, he gave them power to become children of God and believe in his name, who were born not of blood, and not of the will of the flesh, and not of the will of a man, but of God. (John 1:12, 13)

Believing in the name of the Son of God is believing the Word and living by it. The will of the flesh is our own will, which in and of itself is evil; and the will of a man is our own understanding, which in and of itself is false as a result of the evil. Those who are born of these are people who derive what they intend and act and think and speak from their own selves. Those born of God are people who derive what they intend and act and think and speak from the Lord.

In brief, what comes from us is not good. What comes from the Lord is good.

To the Extent That We Turn Our Backs on Evil Deeds Because They Are Sins, the Good Deeds We Do Come Not from Ourselves but from the Lord

IS there anyone who does not and cannot know that our evils stand in the way of the Lord's ability to come in to us? Evil is hell and the Lord is heaven, and hell and heaven are opposites; so to the extent that we are in one we cannot be in the other. One acts against the other and cancels it.

18

19 As long as we are in this world we are in between hell and heaven—hell is below us and heaven above us—and during this time we are kept in a freedom to turn toward hell or toward heaven. If we turn toward hell we are turning away from heaven, while if we turn toward heaven we are turning away from hell.

In other words, as long as we are in this world we are placed in between the Lord and the Devil and are kept in a freedom to turn toward the one or the other. If we turn toward the Devil we turn our backs on the Lord, while if we turn toward the Lord we turn our backs on the Devil.

Or to put it yet another way, as long as we are in this world we are in between what is evil and what is good and are kept in a freedom to turn toward the one or the other. If we turn toward what is evil we turn our backs on what is good, while if we turn toward what is good we turn our backs on what is evil.

20 I have stated that we are kept in a freedom of turning either way. This freedom never comes from us; it comes from the Lord, which is why I just said that we are kept in it.

On the balance between heaven and hell, our being in that balance, and our therefore being in freedom, see *Heaven and Hell* 589–596 and 597–603. As for everyone being kept in freedom and no one being deprived of it, that will come up in its own place [§§101–102].

21 This makes it very clear that to the extent that we turn our backs on evil deeds we are with the Lord and in the Lord; and to the extent that we are in the Lord the good deeds we do come not from ourselves but from the Lord. This yields the following general law: *To the extent that we turn our backs on evil deeds, we do good deeds.*

22 Two things are required, though. First, we need to turn our backs on evil deeds because they are sins—that is, because they are hellish and diabolical and therefore contrary to the Lord and to divine laws. Second, we need to turn our backs on evil deeds because they are sins as if we were doing it on our own, but we need to know and believe that it comes from the Lord. Both of these requirements will be discussed under other headings [§§62–66 and 101–107].

23 There are three corollaries to this.

1. If we intend and do good deeds before we turn our backs on evil deeds because they are sins, our good deeds are not good.
2. If we think and speak devoutly but do not turn our backs on evil deeds because they are sins, our devout thoughts and words are not devout.

3. Even if we are well informed and insightful, if we do not turn our backs on evil deeds because they are sins, we are not wise.

1. *If we intend and do good deeds before we turn our backs on evil deeds because they are sins, our good deeds are not good.* This is because we are not in the Lord yet, as just noted [§21]. For example, if we give to the poor, help the needy, endow churches and hospices, support the church, our country, and our fellow citizens, teach the gospel, make converts, practice justice in judgment, honesty in business, and righteousness in our behavior, but still think nothing of evil like fraud, adultery, hatred, blasphemy, and such things, which are sins, then the only good deeds we can do are inwardly evil. We are doing them on our own behalf, that is, and not on behalf of the Lord. This means that we are inside them and the Lord is not; and any good deeds that have ourselves within them are all polluted by our evils and are focused on ourselves and the world. **24**

However, the same deeds just listed are inwardly good if we are turning from evils because they are sins, evils like fraud, adultery, hatred, blasphemy, and the like. That is, the actions we are doing come from the Lord, and are called *deeds done in God* (John 3:19, 20, 21).

2. *If we think and speak devoutly but do not turn our backs on evil deeds because they are sins, our devout thoughts and words are not devout.* This is because we are not in the Lord. For example, if we attend church regularly, listen reverently to the sermons, read the Word and religious literature, take the Holy Supper, offer our prayers every day, and give a great deal of thought to God and salvation, if we think nothing of evils that are sins—fraud, for example, or adultery, hatred, blasphemy, and the like—then the only devout thought and speech we are capable of is thought and speech that inwardly are not devout at all, because we ourselves with all our evils are within them. We are not aware of this when these acts are happening, but our evils are still in there and are hiding from our sight. It is like a spring whose waters are impure from their source. **25**

At those times our devotional practices are nothing but a routine that has become habitual; or we are thinking highly of ourselves; or we are hypocritical. They do rise up toward heaven, yes, but along the way they turn back and come down the way smoke does in the air.

I have been granted the opportunity to see and hear many people after their deaths listing their good works and their devotional practices along the lines of those just mentioned in §§24 and 25, plus some others as well. I also saw that some of them had lamps but no oil, and when they **26** were asked whether they had turned their backs on evil deeds because they are sins it turned out that they had not. So they were told that they were evil, and later I saw them going into caves where there were other evil people like themselves.

27   *3. Even if we are well informed and insightful, if we do not turn our backs on evil deeds because they are sins, we are not wise.* This too is for the reason just given [§§21, 24, 25], that our wisdom comes from ourselves and not from the Lord. For example, if we know the theology of our church right down to the last detail and know how to support it on the basis of the Word and of reason; if we know the theologies of all the churches through the ages, along with the edicts of all the councils; in fact, if we know truths and see and understand them as well—if, for example, we know what faith is, what caring is, what piety is, what repentance and the forgiveness of sins are, what regeneration is, what baptism and the Holy Supper are, what the Lord is and what redemption and salvation are—we still are not wise unless we turn our backs on evils because they are sins. These are lifeless pieces of information, because they involve only our power of understanding and not at the same time our power of willing. Things like this perish in the course of time for the reasons given in §15 above. After death we ourselves actually discard them because they do not agree with the love that belongs to our will.

All the same, these pieces of information are absolutely necessary because they tell us how we are to behave; and when we do them they come to life for us, but not before.

28   Everything said so far can be found in many places in the Word. I may cite only the following few.

The Word tells us that no one can be focused on doing good and doing evil at the same time, or—which amounts to the same thing—with respect to our souls we cannot be in heaven and in hell at the same time. It tells us this by saying,

> No one can serve two masters; for you will either hate the one and love the other or hold to the one and despise the other. You cannot serve God and Mammon. (Matthew 6:24)

> How can the things you say be good when you are evil? Out of the abundance of the heart the mouth speaks. Good people out of the good treasure of their hearts bring forth good things, and evil people out of the evil treasure bring forth evil things. (Matthew 12:34, 35)

A good tree does not bear bad fruit, and a bad tree does not bear good fruit. Every tree is known by its own fruit. People do not gather figs from thorns or harvest grapes from a bramble bush. (Luke 6:43, 44)

The Word tells us that none of us can do what is good on our own; our actions are good only if they come from the Lord.

> Jesus said, "I am the vine, and my Father is the vinedresser. Every branch in me that does not bear fruit he takes away; and every branch that bears fruit he prunes, so that it will bear more fruit. Abide in me, and I [will abide] in you. As a branch cannot bear fruit on its own unless it abides in the vine, the same goes for you unless you abide in me. I am the vine; you are the branches. Those who abide in me and in whom I abide bear much fruit, because without me you cannot do anything. If any do not abide in me they are cast out as branches and wither; people gather them and throw them into the fire, and they are burned." (John 15:1–6)

The Word tells us in the following passage that to the extent that we are *not* purified from our evils, any good things we do are not good, any devout deeds are not devout, and we are not wise; but the reverse is the case if we *are* purified.

> Woe to you, scribes and Pharisees, hypocrites, because you make yourselves like whitewashed tombs that look beautiful outwardly, but are inwardly full of dead people's bones and filth of every kind. Even so, you look righteous outwardly, but are inwardly full of hypocrisy and iniquity. Woe to you, because you cleanse the outside of the cup and the plate, but inside they are full of extortion and excess. Blind Pharisee, cleanse the inside of the cup and the plate first, so that the outside of them may be clean as well. (Matthew 23:25–28)

Then there are these words of Isaiah:

> Hear the word of Jehovah, you princes of Sodom! Hear the law of our God, you people of Gomorrah! What use to me are your abundant sacrifices? Do not keep bringing worthless offerings! Incense is an abomination to me, your new moons and Sabbaths. I cannot abide iniquity. My soul hates your new moons and prescribed feasts, so when you spread forth your hands I hide my eyes from you. Even though you multiply your prayers, I am not listening—your hands are full of

29

30

blood. Wash yourselves! Purify yourselves! Take away the evil of your
deeds from before my eyes! Stop doing evil! Even if your sins have been
like scarlet, they will become white like snow; even if they have been red,
they will be like wool. (Isaiah 1:10–18)

Put briefly, this is saying that unless we turn our backs on evil deeds,
none of our worship is any good. The same holds true for everything we
do, since it says "I cannot abide iniquity; purify yourselves; take away the
evil of your deeds; stop doing evil." In Jeremiah,

Turn back, all of you, from your evil way, and make your works good.
(Jeremiah 35:15)

[2] These people are not wise, either. See the following from Isaiah:

Woe to those who are wise in their own eyes and intelligent in their
own estimation. (Isaiah 5:21)

Again,

The wisdom of the wise will perish, as will the intelligence of the intelligent. Woe to those whose wisdom is profound and whose deeds are
done in darkness. (Isaiah 29:14, 15)

And yet again,

Woe to those who go down to Egypt for help and who rely on horses,
who trust in an abundance of chariots and in the strength of riders, but
do not look to the Holy One of Israel and do not seek Jehovah. He will
rise up against the house of the malicious and against the aid of those
who work iniquity, because Egypt is not God, and its horses are flesh,
and not spirit. (Isaiah 31:1, 2, 3)

That is how our own intelligence is described. Egypt is mere facts; a horse
is our understanding of those facts; chariots are religious teachings based
on those facts; and riders are the intelligence we develop as a result. Of
these qualities we read, "Woe to those who do not look to the Holy One
of Israel and do not seek Jehovah." "He will rise up against the house of
the malicious and against the aid of those who work iniquity" means the
destruction of these qualities by evils. "Egypt is human, not God, and her
horses are flesh, and not spirit" means that this understanding comes
from our own sense of self-importance and that therefore there is no life
in it. "Human" and "flesh" are our own sense of self, and "God" and

"spirit" are life that comes from the Lord. The horses of Egypt are the intelligence that we claim as our own.

There are many similar passages in the Word whose focus on self-derived intelligence and intelligence that comes from the Lord can be seen only through their spiritual meaning.

[3] We can see from the following passages that none of us can be saved by means of good works done by ourselves, because they are not good.

> Not everyone who says to me, "Lord, Lord," will enter the kingdom of the heavens, but those who do the will of my Father. On that day many will say to me, "Lord, Lord, haven't we prophesied in your name, cast out demons in your name, and done many great things in your name?" But then I will declare to them, "I do not know you. Depart from me, *you workers of iniquity.*" (Matthew 7:21, 22, 23)

And in another passage,

> Then you begin to stand outside and knock on the door, saying, "Lord, open the door for us!" Then you will begin to say, "We ate and drank in your presence, and you taught in our streets." But he will say, "I tell you, I do not know where you are from. Depart from me, all you *workers of iniquity.*" (Luke 13:25, 26, 27)

They are in fact like the Pharisee who prayed, standing in the Temple, saying that he was not greedy, unjust, or adulterous like other people, but fasted twice a week and gave tithes of all he possessed (Luke 18:11–14). They are also the ones called "worthless servants" (Luke 17:10).

The truth is that none of us can on our own do anything good that is really good; but it is outrageous to use this principle to destroy all the good and caring actions done by people who turn away from evils because they are sins. Using this principle in this way is in fact diametrically opposed to the Word, which mandates what we are to do; it is contrary to the commandments of love for the Lord and love for our neighbor on which depend all the Law and the Prophets [Matthew 22:40]; and it is to demean and subvert everything that has to do with religion. Everyone knows that religion means doing what is good and that we are all going to be judged according to our deeds.

We are all by nature capable of turning away from evils with apparent autonomy because of the Lord's power, if we pray for that power; and what we then do is good that comes from the Lord.

To the Extent That We Turn Our Backs on Evils Because They Are Sins, We Love What Is True

32 THERE are two absolutes that emanate from the Lord: divine goodness and divine truth. Divine goodness comes from his divine love, and divine truth comes from his divine wisdom. In the Lord, these two are one and therefore they emanate from him as one. However, they are not received as one by angels in the heavens or by us on earth. There are some angels and people who receive more of divine truth than of divine goodness, and there are others who receive more of divine goodness than of divine truth. That is why the heavens are divided into two kingdoms, one called the heavenly kingdom and the other called the spiritual kingdom. The heavens that receive more of divine goodness form the heavenly kingdom, and the ones that receive more of divine truth form the spiritual kingdom. On these two kingdoms into which the heavens are divided see §§20–28 of *Heaven and Hell*.

[2] Still, the angels of all the heavens enjoy wisdom and intelligence only to the extent that the goodness they practice is united to truth. Any good action of theirs that is not united to truth is for them not actually good; and conversely any truth they possess that is not united to good actions is for them not actually true. We can see from this that goodness united to truth makes love and wisdom for an angel and for us; and since angels are angels because of their love and wisdom, and since the same holds true for us, we can see that goodness united to truth is what makes an angel an angel of heaven and a person a true member of the church.

33 Since what is good and what is true are one in the Lord and emanate from him as one, it follows that goodness loves truth, truth loves goodness, and they want to be one. The same holds true for their opposites. What is evil loves what is false and what is false loves what is evil, and they want to be one. In the following pages the union of goodness and truth will be called "the heavenly marriage" and the union of evil and falsity "the hellish marriage."

34 One consequence of this is that to the extent that we turn our backs on evils because they are sins, we love what is true. That is, we are to that extent focused on what is good, as explained under the previous heading [§§18–31]. Conversely, to the extent that we do not turn our backs on evils because they are sins, we do not love what is true, because to that same extent we are not focused on what is good.

Actually, people who do not turn their backs on evils because they are **35** sins can love what is true. However, they do not love it because it is true but because it enhances their reputation as a means to rank or profit. So if the truth does not enhance their reputation, they do not love it.

Goodness shapes our will, and truth shapes our understanding. From **36** a love for what is good in our will comes a love for what is true in our understanding. From the love for what is true comes a perception of what is true; from a perception of what is true comes thought about what is true; from these comes the recognition of what is true that is faith in its proper definition. It will be shown in the work *Divine Love and Wisdom* that this is how we progress to faith from a love for what is good.

Since goodness is not genuinely good unless it is united to what is true, **37** as noted [§32], it follows that goodness does not become manifest prior to that union, and yet it is constantly trying to become manifest. So in order to become manifest, it longs for and acquires truths for itself. These are the means of its nourishment and its formation. This is why we love what is true to the extent that we are focused on what is good, and accordingly to the same extent that we turn our backs on evils because they are sins; because that determines the extent to which we are focused on what is good.

To the extent that we are focused on what is good and love what is **38** true for the sake of what is good, we are loving the Lord, because the Lord is goodness itself and truth itself. So the Lord is with us in what is good and in what is true. If we love truth for the sake of goodness, then and only then do we love the Lord. This the Lord tells us in John:

> The people who love me are those who have my commandments and do them. Those who do not love me do not keep my words. (John 14:21, 24)

And again,

> If you keep my commandments, you will abide in my love. (John 15:10)

The Lord's words and commandments are truths.

We can illustrate the fact that goodness loves what is true by tak- **39** ing priests, soldiers, merchants, and artisans as examples. With respect to *priests,* if they are focused on the good that a priest can do, which is look- ing out for the salvation of souls, teaching the way to heaven, and leading the people they teach, then because they are focused on this goodness, because they love and long for it, they acquire the truths that they teach and that enable them to lead.

On the other hand, priests who are not focused on the good that priests can do but rather on the gratifications of the office—and who are this way because of love for themselves and for the world, which is all they regard as good—then because of that love and longing they too acquire as much truth as the gratification that is their "goodness" inspires them to acquire.

As for *soldiers,* if they have a love for military service and see some good in it, whether in providing protection or in seeking their own glory, then because of the goodness they seek and in keeping with it they acquire the necessary knowledge and, if they are officers, understanding. These are the truths by which the pleasure of their love, which is their "goodness," is nourished and given form.

As for *merchants,* if they commit themselves to being in business because they love it, they gladly take in everything that serves as a means of putting together and building what they love. These means, too, are like truths, when doing business is the goodness these people love.

As for *artisans,* if they apply themselves to their work diligently and love it as what makes their life worthwhile, they buy their tools and improve themselves by learning what they need to know. This is what makes their work good.

We can see from all this that truths are the means by which the good that we do out of love becomes manifest, becomes something; so goodness loves what is true in order to become manifest.

So in the Word, "doing the truth" means acting in such a way that some good will be done. This is the meaning of "doing the truth" in John 3:21, "doing what the Lord says" in Luke 6:46, "doing his commandments" in John 14:21, "doing his words" in Matthew 7:24, "doing the Word of God" in Luke 8:21, and "doing the statutes and judgments" in Leviticus 18:5.

This is also the meaning of "doing good" and "bearing fruit," because what is done is something "good," some "fruit."

40 We can illustrate the fact that what is good loves what is true and wants to be united to it if we think of food and water or bread and wine. We need both. Food or bread alone does nothing for the nourishment of the body without water or wine, so each seeks for and calls for the other. In fact, in the Word as spiritually understood, food and bread mean what is good, while water and wine mean what is true.

We may conclude from what has been said that if we turn our backs **41**
on evils because they are sins, then we love truths and long for them. The
more resolutely we turn our backs, the more we love and long for truths,
because we are that much more focused on what is good. This is how we
attain the heavenly marriage that is the marriage of goodness and truth,
the marriage in which heaven is and the church should be.

To the Extent That We Turn Our Backs on Evils Because They Are Sins, We Have Faith and Are Spiritual

OUR faith and our life are distinct from each other in the same way **42**
that our thought and our actions are distinct. Since our thinking
comes from our understanding and our actions come from our will, it
follows that our faith and our life are also distinct from each other in the
same way that our understanding and our will are distinct. And therefore
someone who knows how our understanding and our will are distinct
also knows how our faith and our life are distinct; and someone who
knows how our understanding and our will become one also knows how
our faith and our life become one. That is why I need to start with something about understanding and will.

We have two abilities, one called *will* and the other *understanding*. **43**
They can be distinguished from each other, but they were so created as to
be one, and when they are one they are called *the mind*. This means that
they are the human mind; they are the home of all that is alive in us. Just
as all things in the universe (those that agree with the divine design) trace
their origin back to goodness and truth, so everything in us traces its
origin back to our will and our understanding. This is because whatever
is good in us resides in our will and whatever is true in us resides in our
understanding. These two faculties receive and are acted upon by what
is good and true: our will is what receives and is acted upon by anything

that is good, and our understanding is what receives and is acted upon by anything that is true. Further, since what is good and what is true in us are not to be found anywhere else, neither are love and faith, since love and goodness are mutually dependent, and so are faith and truth.

[2] There is no knowledge more relevant than knowing how our will and understanding make one mind. They make one mind the way goodness and truth make a single reality. There is the same kind of marriage between will and understanding as there is between what is good and what is true. You can catch a glimpse of what that marriage is like from what has just been presented under the previous heading [§§32–41]; to which I should add that just as everything has goodness as its underlying reality and truth as its consequent manifestation, so our will is the underlying reality of our life and our understanding is its consequent manifestation. This is because any instance of goodness that comes from our will takes form in our understanding and makes itself visible to us there in some specific way.

44   I explained in §§27–28 above that we can know a great deal, can think and understand, and still not be wise; and since faith involves knowing and thinking and especially understanding that something is so, we can believe that we have faith although in fact we do not. The reason we do not have faith is that we are leading an evil life, and there is no way that an evil life and the truth we believe can act in unison. The evil we practice destroys the truth we believe. This is because the evil we practice resides in our will, but the truth we believe resides in our understanding; and will leads understanding and makes it act in unison with itself. So if there is anything in our understanding that does not agree with our will, when we are left to ourselves and are thinking on the basis of our evil and its love, then we either discard the truth that is in our understanding or make it cooperate by distorting it.

It is different if we are leading a good life. Then when we are left to ourselves we think on the basis of what is good, and love the truth that is in our understanding because it agrees. So there is a union of faith and life like the union of what is true and what is good, and both the former and the latter are like the union between understanding and will.

45   It then follows that as we turn our backs on evils because they are sins we have faith, because as explained just above this means that we are focused on what is good. There is support for this in the contrasting fact that if we do not turn our backs on evils because they are sins we do not have faith, because we are focused on what is evil, and evil has an intrinsic hatred for truth. Outwardly, yes, we can befriend truth and put up with it and even love having it in our understanding; but when we shed that outwardness, as happens after death, we first discard the truth we befriended in the world, then we deny that it is true, and finally we turn away from it.

When we are evil, our faith is an intellectual faith that has nothing good in it from our will. As a result, it is a dead faith that is like breathing with our lungs but without any life from our heart (our understanding corresponds to our lungs and our will corresponds to our heart). It is also like an alluring whore, decked out with rouge and jewels, who has a virulent disease within. In fact, whores correspond to the distortion of what is true and therefore have that meaning in the Word. **46**

It is also like a tree with lush foliage that does not bear fruit, a tree that the gardener cuts down. A tree stands for a person, too, its flowers and leaves meaning the truths we believe and its fruit meaning our love for doing good.

But the faith residing in our understanding is different if it has within itself a goodness that comes from our will. It is alive and is like the breathing of our lungs that has its life from our heart. It is also like an attractive wife who is loved by her husband because of her chastity, and like a tree that is fruitful.

There are many things that seem to require faith only, such as the existence of God, the Lord who is God being our Redeemer and Savior, the reality of heaven and hell, life after death, and any number of other issues. We describe them not as things to be done but as things to be believed. Yet even these matters of faith are dead if we are focused on what is evil, but alive if we are focused on what is good. **47**

This is because when we are focused on what is good we not only behave well because of our will but also think well because of our understanding; this not only in front of others, in public, but also in our own sight, when we are alone. It is different when we are focused on what is evil.

As just mentioned, these beliefs seem to require faith only. But the thinking in our understanding is a manifestation of the love that belongs to our will; that love is the underlying reality of the thinking in our understanding (see §43 above). That is, if we will to do something because of love, we want to do it—we want to think it, we want to understand it, and we want to say it. Or in other words, whatever we love because of intent we love to do, we love to think, we love to understand, and we love to say. **48**

Then too, when we turn our backs on evils because they are sins we are in the Lord, as explained above [§§18–31], and the Lord is doing everything. That is why the Lord said to those who were asking him what they should do in order to work the works of God, "This is the work of God, that you believe in the one whom he has sent" (John 6:29). Believing in the Lord is not simply thinking that he exists but is also doing what he says, as he tells us elsewhere [Matthew 7:24].

49   People who are caught up in evil do not have any faith even though they believe that they do, as I have been shown by seeing some people of this sort in the spiritual world. They were brought into a heavenly community, which caused the spiritual side of the angels' faith to enter into the deeper levels of the faith of the visitors. This made the visitors aware of the fact that all they had was an earthly or outward faith and not its spiritual or inner side. So they themselves admitted that they had no faith whatever and that in the world they had convinced themselves that if they thought something was true for any reason at all, that was "believing" or "having faith."

The faith of people who have not been devoted to evil, though, looks very different.

50   This shows us what a spiritual faith is and what a nonspiritual faith is. Spiritual faith is characteristic of people who do not commit sins, because the good actions of people who do not commit sins come from the Lord and not from themselves (see §§18–31 above); and through their faith they become spiritual. For them, faith is truth.

This is how the Lord says it in John:

> This is the condemnation, that light has come into the world, but people loved darkness rather than light, because their deeds were evil. All who do evil hate the light and do not come to the light, or else their deeds would be exposed; but those who do the truth come to the light so that their deeds may be clearly seen, because their deeds were done in God. (John 3:19, 20, 21)

51   The following passages support what has been said thus far:

> Good people out of the good treasure of their hearts bring forth what is good; evil people out of the evil treasure of their hearts bring forth what is evil. Out of the abundance of the heart the mouth speaks. (Luke 6:45; Matthew 12:35)

In the Word, the heart means our will, and since this is the source of our thinking and speaking, it says that "out of the abundance of the heart the mouth speaks."

> It is not what goes into the mouth that makes people unclean but what comes out of the heart; this is what makes people unclean. (Matthew 15:11)

Again, the heart means our will. And Jesus said of the woman who had washed his feet with anointing oil that her sins were forgiven because she loved greatly; and later added, "Your faith is saving you" (Luke 7:46–50).

We can see from these words that when our sins are forgiven—that is, when they are no longer there—our faith saves us.

In John 1:12, 13 the Lord tells us that people are called "children of God" and "born of God" when their will is not full of a sense of self-importance and their understanding is therefore not clouded by that same sense of self-importance—that is, when they are not focused on what is evil and therefore on what is false. He also teaches us there that such people are the ones who believe in the Lord. For an explanation of these verses see the end of §17 above.

The conclusion follows from this that there is not the slightest bit **52** more of truth in us than there is of what is good, so there is not the slightest bit of faith than there is of life. The knowledge that something is so may exist in our understanding, but unless our will agrees, that knowledge is not the acknowledgment that constitutes faith. So faith and life walk side by side.

This now allows us to see that to the extent we turn our backs on evils because they are sins, we have faith and are spiritual.

The Ten Commandments Tell Us Which Evils Are Sins

IS there any society anywhere on the globe that does not know that it **53** is evil to steal, commit adultery, murder, and bear false witness? If they did not know this, and if they were not prevented by laws from doing these things, it would be all over for them, because any community or republic or kingdom would collapse if it did not have these laws. Could anyone presume that the Israelite nation was so much more stupid than everyone else that they did not know these things were evil? So we might wonder why these laws, so well known over the whole face of the earth, were made public by Jehovah himself from Mount Sinai in such miraculous fashion.

But the truth is that they were made public in such miraculous fashion to let Israel know that these laws are not merely civil and moral laws but are spiritual laws as well, and that breaking them is not only harmful to our fellow citizens and communities but is also a sin against God. So the proclamation of these laws from Mount Sinai by Jehovah made them laws of religion. It is obvious that if Jehovah God commands something, he does so in order to make it a part of our religion, as something that needs to be done for his sake and for the sake of our own salvation.

54 Because these laws were the very beginnings of the Word and therefore of the church that the Lord was establishing with the Israelite people, and because they brought together in a brief summary all the elements of religion that make possible the Lord's union with us and our union with the Lord, they were so holy that nothing is holier.

55 We can tell how supremely holy they were from the fact that Jehovah himself—the Lord, that is—came down upon Mount Sinai in fire, with angels, and proclaimed them from there with his own voice, and that the people spent three days preparing themselves for seeing and hearing all this. The mountain was also fenced off so that no one would approach it and die. Not even priests or elders were allowed near; Moses alone was allowed. The laws were written on two stone tablets by the finger of God. When Moses brought the tablets down from the mountain the second time, his face shone. Later they were placed in an ark, which was set in the very heart of the tabernacle and had a mercy seat on it, with angel guardians made of gold above that. There was nothing holier in their church, and it was called "the most holy place." Outside the veil that surrounded it they brought together things that represented holy elements of heaven and the church—the lampstand with its seven golden lamps, the golden altar of incense, and the gilded table for the showbread, all surrounded by curtains of fine linen and purple and scarlet thread. The sole reason for the holiness of this whole tabernacle was the law that was in the ark.

[2] Because of the holiness of the tabernacle, which resulted from the presence of the law in the ark, the whole Israelite population camped around it, in a set arrangement tribe by tribe, and traveled behind it in a set sequence. There was also a cloud above it in the daytime then, and

fire above it at night. Because of the holiness of the law and the Lord's presence in it, it was upon the mercy seat between the angel guardians that the Lord spoke to Moses, and the ark was called "Jehovah" there. In fact Aaron was not allowed to go behind the veil without sacrifices and incense.

Because the law was the essential holiness of the church, David brought the ark into Zion, and it was later placed at the center of the Jerusalem temple where [Solomon] had made an inner sanctuary for it.

[3] Because of the Lord's presence in and around the law, miracles were performed by means of the ark in which the law lay. For example, the waters of the Jordan were cut off, and as long as the ark rested in its midst, the people crossed over on dry ground. The walls of Jericho fell because the ark was carried around them. Dagon, the god of the Philistines, fell before the ark and later lay on the threshold of the shrine with its head broken off. Tens of thousands of the people of Beth-shemesh were struck down because of the ark, and so on. All these things happened simply because of the Lord's presence in his "Ten Words," which are the Ten Commandments.

Another reason for the power and holiness of that law is that it is a **56** summary of everything that constitutes religion. That is, it consisted of two tablets, one briefly containing everything that has to do with God and the other everything that has to do with us. That is why the commandments of that law are called "the Ten Words"—so called because "ten" means "all."

How that law summarizes everything that constitutes religion, though, will be explained under the next heading [§64].

Because that law is the means of the Lord's union with us and our **57** union with the Lord, it is called a *covenant* and a *testimony*—a covenant because it unites and a testimony because it bears witness.

That is why there were two tablets, one for the Lord and one for us. The union is effected by the Lord, but it is effected when we do what is written on our tablet. That is, the Lord is constantly present and active and wanting to come in, but because of the freedom he gives us, it is up to us to open [the door], for he says,

Behold, I stand at the door and knock. If any hear my voice and open the door, I will come in to them and dine with them and they with me. (Revelation 3:20)

In the second tablet, which is for us, it does not say that we must **58** do some specific good thing but that we must not do some specific evil thing—for example, "You are not to kill, you are not to commit adultery, you are not to steal, you are not to bear false witness, you are not to covet." This is because we cannot do anything good on our own, but when we do not do evil things, the good things we do come not from ourselves but from the Lord.

We shall see in what follows [§§101–107] that we can turn our backs on evil—seemingly on our own, but actually with the Lord's power—if we ask for this humbly.

59 The statements made in §55 above about the proclamation, holiness, and power of the law may be found in the following passages in the Word: Jehovah came down in fire upon Mount Sinai and the mountain smoked and shook; and there was thunder, lightning, thick clouds, and the sound of a trumpet (Exodus 19:16, 18; Deuteronomy 4:11; 5:22–23). Before Jehovah came down, the people spent three days preparing and sanctifying themselves (Exodus 19:10, 11, 15). The mountain was fenced off so that no one would approach and come near its base and die; not even priests were allowed near; Moses alone was allowed (Exodus 19:12, 13, 20–23; 24:1, 2). The law was proclaimed from Mount Sinai (Exodus 20:2–17; Deuteronomy 5:6–21). The law was written on two stone tablets by the finger of God (Exodus 31:18; 32:15, 16; Deuteronomy 9:10). When Moses brought the tablets down from the mountain the second time, his face shone (Exodus 34:29–35). The tablets were placed in an ark (Exodus 25:16; 40:20; Deuteronomy 10:5; 1 Kings 8:9). On top of the ark there was a mercy seat, and on the mercy seat were placed angel guardians made of gold (Exodus 25:17–21). The ark, with the mercy seat and the angel guardians, formed the very heart of the tabernacle, while the golden lampstand, the golden altar of incense, and the gilded table for the showbread were placed just outside [the veil], and all these objects were surrounded in turn by the ten curtains of fine linen and purple and scarlet [thread] (Exodus 25:1 to the end; 26:1 to the end; 40:17–28). The area set aside for the ark was called "the most holy place" (Exodus 26:33). The whole Israelite population camped around the dwelling, in a set arrangement tribe by tribe, and traveled behind it in a set sequence (Numbers 2:1 to the end). There was a cloud above the tabernacle in the daytime then, and fire above it at night (Exodus 40:38; Numbers 9:15, 16 to the end; 14:14; Deuteronomy 1:33). The Lord spoke with Moses from above the ark, between the angel guardians (Exodus 25:22; Numbers 7:89). Because it contained the law, the ark was called "Jehovah" there: when the ark would set out, Moses would say, "Rise up, Jehovah," and when it would come to rest he would say, "Return, Jehovah" (Numbers 10:35, 36; see also 2 Samuel 6:2 and Psalms 132:7, 8). Because of the holiness of the law, Aaron was not allowed to go behind the veil without sacrifices and incense (Leviticus 16:2–14 and following). David brought the ark into Zion with sacrifices and rejoicing (2 Samuel 6:1–19). At that time Uzzah died because he touched the ark (2 Samuel 6:6, 7). [Solomon] placed the ark at the center of the Jerusalem temple, where he had made an inner sanctuary for it (1 Kings 6:19 and following; 8:3–9). Because of the Lord's presence and power in the law that was in the ark, the waters of the Jordan were cut off; and as long as the ark rested in its midst, the people crossed over on dry ground (Joshua 3:1–17; 4:5–20). The walls of Jericho fell because the ark was carried around them (Joshua 6:1–20). Dagon, the god of the Philistines, fell to the earth before the ark and later lay on the threshold of the shrine with its head broken off (1 Samuel 5:1–4). Tens of thousands of the people of Beth-shemesh were struck down because of the ark (1 Samuel 6:19).

The stone tablets on which the law was written were called "the tablets of the covenant," and because of them the ark was called "the ark of the covenant" and the law itself was called "the covenant" (Numbers 10:33; Deuteronomy 4:13, 23; 5:2, 3; 9:9; Joshua 3:11; 1 Kings 8:21; Revelation 11:19; and often elsewhere). **60**

The reason the law was called the covenant is that "covenant" means union. That is why it says of the Lord that he will be "a covenant for the people" (Isaiah 42:6; 49:8); why he is called "the angel of the covenant" (Malachi 3:1); and why his blood is called "the blood of the covenant" (Matthew 26:28; Zechariah 9:11; Exodus 24:4–10). That is why the Word is called "the Old Covenant" and "the New Covenant."

Covenants are made for the sake of love, friendship, and companionship, and therefore for the sake of union.

The commandments of the law were called "the ten words" (Exodus 34:28; Deuteronomy 4:13; 10:4). This is because "ten" means all and "words" means truths. After all, there were more than ten. **61**

Because "ten" means all, there were ten curtains of the tabernacle (Exodus 26:1). That is why the Lord said that the one who was going to receive a kingdom called ten servants and gave them ten minas for doing business (Luke 19:13). It is why the Lord compared the kingdom of the heavens to ten young women (Matthew 25:1), and why the dragon is described as having ten horns (Revelation 12:3). The same holds true for the beast rising up out of the sea (Revelation 13:1), and the other beast

(Revelation 17:3, 7), as well as the beast in Daniel (Daniel 7:7, 20, 24). "Ten" means the same in Leviticus 26:26, Zechariah 8:23, and elsewhere. That is where "tithes" come from, meaning some portion of all.

All Kinds of Murder, Adultery, Theft, and False Witness, Together with Urges toward Them, Are Evils on Which We Must Turn Our Backs Because They Are Sins

62 IT is common knowledge that the law of Sinai was written on two tablets and that the first tablet contains matters concerning God and the second, matters concerning us. It is not obvious in the literal text that the first tablet contains everything to do with God and that the second contains everything to do with us, but it is all in there. It is actually why they are called "the ten words," meaning all truths in summary (see §61 just above). However, there is no way to explain briefly how everything is there, though it can be grasped by reference to what is presented in §67 of *Teachings on Sacred Scripture,* which the reader may consult.

This is the reason for mentioning "*all kinds* of murder, adultery, theft, and false witness."

63 The prevailing religious belief holds that no one can fulfill the law. And [yet] the law demands that we must not kill, commit adultery, steal, or bear false witness. Any civic and moral individual can fulfill these elements of the law by living a good civic and moral life; but this religious belief denies that we can do so by living a good spiritual life. This leads to the conclusion that our reason for not committing these crimes is simply to avoid punishment and loss in this world, but not to avoid punishment and loss after we leave this world. The result is that people who hold this conviction think that immoral actions are permissible in the eyes of God but not in the eyes of the world.

[2] Because of the kind of thinking that is based on this religious principle, people have cravings to commit all these evils; for worldly reasons only, they forgo doing them. So even if they have not committed murder, adultery, theft, or false witness, after death people like this still feel the urge to commit such sins; and they actually do when they lose the outer facade they had in the world. All our cravings await us after death. This is why people like this act in concert with hell and cannot help suffering the same fate as people in hell.

[3] Things turn out differently, though, if we do not want to murder, commit adultery, steal, or bear false witness, because such behavior is contrary to God. Once we have fought against them to some extent we do not intend them, so we feel no urge to do them. We say in our hearts that they are sins, essentially hellish and diabolic. Then after death, when we lose any facade we maintained for worldly reasons, we act in concert with heaven; and because we are focused on the Lord, we also enter heaven.

Every religion has the general principle that we are to examine ourselves, practice repentance, and refrain from sins, and if we do not do this, we suffer damnation. (See above, §§1–8, on this being a common feature of all religion.)   **64**

The whole Christian world also has the common practice of teaching the Ten Commandments as a way of introducing little children to the Christian religion. These commandments are in every little child's hand. Their parents and teachers tell them that doing such things is sinning against God. In fact, when they talk with children they have no other thought in their heads but this. It is little short of amazing that these same people, and the children when they grow up, think that they are not subject to the law and that they are incapable of doing what the law requires. Can there be any reason why they learn to think like this other than that they love evils and therefore love the false notions that support them? These are the individuals, then, who do not regard the Ten Commandments as matters of religion. See *Teachings on Faith* on the fact that there is no religion in the lives of such people.

Every society on the face of the whole earth that has any religion has laws like the Ten Commandments, and all the individuals who live by them as a matter of religion are saved, while all who do not live by them as a matter of religion are damned. After death, the ones who have lived by them as a matter of religion are taught by angels, accept truths, and acknowledge the Lord. This is because they have turned their backs on   **65** evils because they are sins and have therefore been devoted to doing what is good, and their resulting goodness loves truth and eagerly drinks it in (see §§32–41 above).

This is the meaning of the Lord's words to the Jews:

> The kingdom of God will be taken from you and given to a nation that bears fruit. (Matthew 21:43)

And also these words:

> When the lord of the vineyard comes, he will destroy those evil people and lease his vineyard to other farmers who will give him its fruits in their season. (Matthew 21:40, 41)

And these:

> I tell you that many will come from the east and the west, and from the north and the south, and will sit down in the kingdom of God, but the children of the kingdom will be cast out into outer darkness. (Matthew 8:11, 12; Luke 13:29)

66   We read in Mark that a certain rich man came to Jesus and asked him what he needed to do in order to inherit eternal life. Jesus said, "You know the commandments: you are not to commit adultery; you are not to kill; you are not to steal; you are not to bear false witness; you are not to commit fraud; honor your father and mother." He replied, "Since my youth I have kept all these things." Jesus looked at him and loved him, but said, "One thing you lack: Go, sell whatever you have and give to the poor, and you will have treasure in the heavens; and come, take up the cross, and follow me" (Mark 10:17–22).

[2] It says that Jesus loved him, and this was because he had kept the commandments since his youth. Because he lacked three things, though—he had not detached his heart from wealth, he had not fought against his cravings, and he had not yet acknowledged the Lord as God— the Lord told him that he was to sell everything he had, meaning that he was to detach his heart from wealth; that he was to take up the cross, meaning that he was to fight against his cravings; and that he was to follow him, meaning that he was to acknowledge the Lord as God. The Lord said these things the way he said everything else—in correspondences (see *Teachings on Sacred Scripture* 17). The fact is that we—and this means everyone—cannot turn our backs on evils because they are sins unless we acknowledge the Lord and turn to him, and unless we fight against evils, and in this way distance ourselves from our cravings.

More on this, though, under the heading concerning doing battle against evils [§§92–100].

To the Extent That We Turn Our Backs on All Kinds of Killing Because They Are Sins, We Have Love for Our Neighbor

ALL kinds of killing means all kinds of hostility, hatred, and vengefulness, which yearn for murder. Killing lies hidden within such attitudes like fire that smolders beneath the ashes. That is exactly what hellfire is. It is why we say that people are on fire with hatred and burning for vengeance. These are types of killing in an earthly sense; but in a spiritual sense "killing" means all of the many and varied ways of killing and destroying people's souls. Then in the highest sense it means harboring hatred for the Lord. **67**

These three kinds of killing align and are united, since anyone who intends the physical murder of someone in this world intends the murder of that individual's soul after death and intends the murder of the Lord, actually burning with hatred against him and wanting to eradicate his name.

These kinds of killing lie hidden within us from birth, but from early childhood we learn to veil them with the civility and morality we need when we are with others in this world; and to the extent that we yearn for rank or money, we take care not to let them become visible. This latter character becomes our outside, while the former is our inside and is what we are like in and of ourselves; so you can see how demonic we will be after death, when we put off that outside along with our bodies, unless we have been reformed. **68**

Since the kinds of killing just mentioned lie hidden within us from birth, as noted, along with all kinds of theft and all kinds of false witness and the urges to commit them (which will be described shortly [§§80–86, **69**

87–91]), we can see that if the Lord had not provided means of reformation, we would inevitably perish forever.

The means of reformation that the Lord has provided are the following: we are born into utter ignorance; as newborns we are kept in a state of outward innocence; soon thereafter we are kept in a state of outward caring and then in a state of outward friendship. But as we become capable of thinking with our own intellect, we are kept in some freedom to act rationally. This is the state described in §19 above, and I need to turn back to it at this point for the sake of what will follow.

As long as we are in this world we are in between hell and heaven—hell is below us and heaven above us—and during this time we are kept in a freedom to turn toward hell or toward heaven. If we turn toward hell we are turning away from heaven, while if we turn toward heaven we are turning away from hell.

In other words, as long as we are in this world we are placed in between the Lord and the Devil and are kept in a freedom to turn toward the one or the other. If we turn toward the Devil we turn our backs on the Lord, while if we turn toward the Lord we turn our backs on the Devil.

Or to put it yet another way, as long as we are in this world we are in between what is evil and what is good and are kept in a freedom to turn toward the one or the other. If we turn toward what is evil we turn our backs on what is good, while if we turn toward what is good we turn our backs on what is evil.

This you will find in §19; see also §§20, 21, and 22, which follow it.

70 Now, since what is evil and what is good are two opposite things, like hell and heaven or like the Devil and the Lord, it follows that if we turn our backs on something evil as a sin we come into something good that is the opposite of that evil. The goodness that is opposite to the evil meant by killing is loving our neighbor.

71 Since this goodness and that evil are opposites, it follows that the latter is repelled by the former. Two opposites cannot be one, as heaven and hell cannot be one. If they did, it would be like that lukewarm state described in the Book of Revelation as follows:

> I know that you are neither cold nor hot. It would have been better if you were cold or hot; but since you are lukewarm and neither cold nor hot, I am about to vomit you out of my mouth. (Revelation 3:15, 16)

72 When we are no longer caught up in the evil of killing but are moved by the good we do out of love for our neighbor, then whatever we do is something good that results from that love, so it is a good work. Priests who are engaged in this goodness are doing a good work whenever they teach and lead because it comes from a love for saving souls. People in administrative roles who are engaged in this goodness are doing a good work whenever they make arrangements and decisions because it comes from a love for serving the country, the community, and their fellow citizens. By the same token, if merchants are engaged in this goodness all of their business is a good work. There is love for their neighbor within it, and their neighbor is the country, the community, their fellow citizens, and their own households as well, whose well-being concerns them as much as their own does. Laborers who are devoted to this goodness do their work faithfully because of it, acting as much for others as for themselves, and being as fearful of harming others as of harming themselves.

The reason their actions are good deeds is that to the extent that we turn our backs on anything evil we do something good, in keeping with the general principle presented above in §21; and anyone who turns away from something evil as a sin is doing what is good not because of his or her self but because of the Lord (see §§18–31).

On the contrary, if we do not regard all kinds of killing—hostility, hatred, vengeance, and the like—as sins, then whether we are priests, administrators, merchants, or laborers, no matter what we do it is not a good deed, because everything we do shares in the evil that is within it. It is in fact what is inside that is producing it. The outside may be good, but only for others, not for ourselves.

The Lord teaches good and loving actions in many passages in the Word. He teaches such actions in Matthew when he instructs us to be reconciled with our neighbor: **73**

> If you bring your gift to the altar and in doing so remember that your brother or sister has something against you, leave your gift there in front of the altar. First be reconciled with your brother or sister, and then come and offer your gift. And be kind and generous to your adversary when you are both on the way [to court], to keep your adversary from turning you over to a judge, keep the judge from turning you over to an officer, and keep you from being thrown in prison. I tell you in truth, you will not be released until you have paid the last penny. (Matthew 5:23–26)

Being reconciled with our brother or sister is turning our backs on hostility, hatred, and vengefulness. We can see that this is turning our backs on these evils because they are sins.

The Lord also tells us in Matthew,

Whatever you want people to do for you, you do the same for them. This is the Law and the Prophets. (Matthew 7:12)

[We should do] nothing evil, then; and [this is said] quite often elsewhere. Then too, the Lord tells us that killing is also being angry with our sister or brother or neighbor for no good reason and harboring hatred against them (see Matthew 5:21, 22).

To the Extent That We Turn Our Backs on All Kinds of Adultery Because They Are Sins, We Love Chastity

74 UNDERSTOOD on an earthly level, the adultery named in the sixth commandment means not only acts of fornication but also lecherous behavior, lewd conversation, and filthy thoughts. Understood on a spiritual level, though, adultery means polluting what is good in the Word and distorting what is true in it, while understood on the highest level it means denying the divine nature of the Lord and profaning the Word. These are "all kinds of adultery."

On the basis of rational light, earthly-minded people can know that "adultery" also means lecherous behavior, lewd conversation, and filthy thoughts, but not that adultery means polluting what is good in the Word and distorting what is true in it, and certainly not that it means denying the divine nature of the Lord and profaning the Word. So they do not know that adultery is so evil that it can be called the height of wickedness. This is because anyone who is intent on earthly adultery is also intent on spiritual adultery, and the reverse. This will be shown in a separate booklet on marriage. But in fact, people whose faith and way of life do not lead them to regard adultery as a sin are engaged in the totality of adultery at every moment.

The reason people love marriage to the extent that they turn their backs on adultery—or to be more precise, love the chastity of marriage to the extent that they turn their backs on the lechery of adultery—is that the lechery of adultery and the chastity of marriage are two opposite things. This means that to the extent that we are not intent on the one we are intent on the other. This is exactly like what has been said in §70 above. **75**

We cannot know the true nature of the chastity of marriage if we do not turn our backs on the lechery of adultery as a sin. We can know something we have experienced, but not something that we have not experienced. If we know about something we have not experienced, know it on the basis of a description or by thinking about it, we know it only in the shadows, and doubt clings to it. So we see it in the light and without doubt only when we have experienced it. This is knowing, then; the other is knowing and yet not knowing. **76**

The truth of the matter is that the lechery of adultery and the chastity of marriage are as different from each other as hell and heaven are from each other, and that the lechery of adultery makes hell for us and the chastity of marriage makes heaven for us.

However, there is no chastity of marriage for anyone but those who turn their backs on adultery as a sin—see §111 below.

This enables us to conclude and see beyond doubt whether someone is a Christian or not, in fact whether or not someone has any religion at all. People who do not regard adultery as a sin in their faith and their way of life are not Christians and have no religion. On the other hand, people who turn their backs on adultery as a sin, and more so people who steer clear of it altogether for that reason, and even more so people who detest it for that reason, do have a religion, and if they are in the Christian church, they are Christians. **77**

There will be more on this in the booklet on marriage, though; and in the meanwhile those interested may consult what it says on this subject in *Heaven and Hell* 366–386.

We can tell from what the Lord says in Matthew that adultery also means lecherous behavior, lewd conversation, and filthy thoughts: **78**

> You have heard that it was said by the ancients, "You are not to commit adultery"; but I tell you that anyone who has looked at someone else's wife in order to desire her has already committed adultery with her in his heart. (Matthew 5:27, 28)

79 The following passages show that spiritually understood, "adultery" means polluting what is good in the Word and distorting what is true in it:

> Babylon has made all nations drink of the wine of her fornication. (Revelation 14:8)

> An angel said, "I will show you the judgment of the great whore who sits on many waters, with whom the kings of the earth committed fornication." (Revelation 17:1, 2)

> Babylon has made all nations drink of the wine of the wrath of her fornication, and the kings of the earth have committed fornication with her. (Revelation 18:3)

> God has judged the great whore who corrupted the earth with her fornication. (Revelation 19:2)

Fornication is associated with Babylon because Babylon means people who claim the Lord's divine power for themselves and profane the Word by polluting and distorting it. That is why Babylon is called "the Mother of Fornications and of the Abominations of the Earth" in Revelation 17:5.

[2] Fornication means much the same in the prophets—in Jeremiah, for example:

> In the prophets of Jerusalem I have seen appalling obstinacy; they commit adultery and walk in a lie. (Jeremiah 23:14)

In Ezekiel:

> Two women, daughters of one mother, played the whore in Egypt; in their youth they behaved wantonly. The first was unfaithful to me and took delight in lovers from neighboring Assyria. Upon them, too, she bestowed her acts of whoredom, but without giving up her wantonness in Egypt. The second became more corrupt in her love than the first, and her acts of whoredom were worse than her sister's. She increased her whoredom and made love to Chaldeans; sons of Babel came to her, into the bed of love, and defiled her with their debauchery. (Ezekiel 23:2–17)

This is about the church of Israel and Judah, who are the "daughters of one mother" in this passage. Their acts of whoredom mean their pollutions and distortions of the Word, and since in the Word Egypt means factual knowledge, Assyria reasoning, Chaldea the profanation of what is true, and Babel the profanation of what is good, it says that they committed acts of whoredom with those countries.

[3] Much the same is said in Ezekiel of Jerusalem, meaning the church in respect to its teachings:

> Jerusalem, you trusted in your own beauty, and played the whore because of your fame, even to the point that you poured out your whoredom on everyone who passed by. You played the whore with the Egyptians, your very fleshly neighbors, and increased your acts of whoredom. You played the whore with the Assyrians, because you were insatiable; indeed you played the whore with them. You multiplied your acts of whoredom as far as the land of the trader, Chaldea. An adulterous wife takes strangers instead of her husband. All make payment to their whores, but you made payments to all your lovers to come to you from all around for your whoredom. Now then, O whore, hear the Word of Jehovah. (Ezekiel 16:15, 26, 28, 29, 32, 33, 35, and following)

On Jerusalem meaning the church, see *Teachings on the Lord* 62, 63. Fornication means much the same in Isaiah 23:17, 18; 57:3; Jeremiah 3:2, 6, 8, 9; 5:7; 13:27; 29:23; Micah 1:7; Nahum 3:4; Hosea 4:7, 10, 11; also Leviticus 20:5; Numbers 14:33; 15:39; and elsewhere.

That is why the Lord called the Jewish nation "an adulterous generation" (Matthew 12:39; 16:4; Mark 8:38).

To the Extent That We Turn Our Backs on All Kinds of Theft Because They Are Sins, We Love Honesty

IN earthly terms, "theft" means not only theft and robbery but also **80** cheating and taking other people's assets by some pretext. Spiritually understood, though, "theft" means depriving others of the truths of their faith and good actions motivated by their caring, while in the highest sense it means taking from the Lord what is properly his and claiming it for ourselves—that is, claiming righteousness and worth for ourselves. These are "all kinds of theft," and like "all kinds of adultery" and "all kinds of killing," as just described [§§74–79 and §§67–73], they too are united. They are united because one is within the other.

81 The evil of theft infects us more deeply than some other evils because it is united with guile and trickery, and guile and trickery work their way into our spiritual mind where our thinking with understanding takes place. We shall see below that we have a spiritual mind and an earthly mind [§86].

82 The reason we love honesty to the extent that we turn our backs on theft as a sin is that theft is also deception, and deception and honesty are two opposite things. This means that to the extent that we are not devoted to deception, we are devoted to honesty.

83 "Honesty" also means integrity, fairness, faithfulness, and morality. On our own, we cannot be devoted to these so as to love them for what they are, for their own sakes, but if we turn our backs on deception, guile, and trickery as sins, we have a devotion to these virtues that comes not from ourselves but from the Lord, as explained in §§18–31 above. This applies to priests, administrators, judges, merchants, and laborers— to all of us then, in our various roles and tasks.

84 There are many passages in the Word that say this, the following being a few of them:

> Those who walk in righteousness and say what is upright, who loathe oppression for the sake of profit, who shake bribes from their hands in order not to accept them, who block their ears so as not to hear blood-shed, who close their eyes so as not to see evil—they will dwell on high. (Isaiah 33:15, 16)

> Jehovah, who will dwell in your tabernacle? Who will live on your holy mountain? Those who walk uprightly and do what is fair, who do not disparage others with their tongues, and who do no evil to their companions. (Psalms 15:1, 2, 3, and following)

> My eyes are toward the faithful of the earth so that they may sit down with me. Anyone who walks the path of integrity will serve me. No one who practices deceit will sit in the midst of my house; no one who speaks lies will stand in my presence. At dawn I will cut off all the

ungodly of the earth, to cut off from the city all those who work iniquity. (Psalms 101:6, 7, 8)

[2] In the following words, the Lord tells us that we are not truly honest, fair, faithful, or upright until we are inwardly honest, fair, faithful, and upright:

> Unless your righteousness exceeds that of the scribes and Pharisees, you will not enter the kingdom of the heavens. (Matthew 5:20)

Righteousness that exceeds that of the scribes and Pharisees means the more inward righteousness that is ours when we are in the Lord. As for our being "in the Lord," he also teaches this in John:

> The glory that you gave me I have given them, so that they may be one just as we are one—I in them and you in me—so that they may be made perfect in one, and so that the love with which you loved me may be in them, and I may be in them. (John 17:22, 23, 26)

This shows that people become complete when the Lord is in them. These are the people who are called "pure in heart," the ones who "will see God," and the ones who are "perfect, like their Father in the heavens" (Matthew 5:8, 48).

I noted in §81 above that the evil of theft infects us more deeply than some other evils because it is united with guile and trickery, and guile and trickery work their way into our spiritual mind where our thinking with understanding takes place; so now I need to say something about the human *mind.* On the human mind being our understanding together with our will, see §43 above.   **85**

We have an earthly mind and a spiritual mind, the earthly mind below and the spiritual mind above. The earthly mind is our mind for this world and the spiritual mind is our mind for heaven. The earthly mind can be called the animal mind, while the spiritual mind can be called the human mind. We are differentiated from animals by our having a spiritual mind that makes it possible for us to be in heaven while we are in this world. It is also what makes it possible for us to live after death.   **86**

[2] We can use our faculty of understanding to be in the spiritual side of our mind, and thus to be in heaven, but we cannot use our faculty of willing to be so unless we turn our backs on evils because they are sins;

and if our will is not in heaven as well [as our understanding], we ourselves are still not there, because our will drags our understanding back down and makes it just as earthly and animal as itself.

[3] We can be compared to a garden, our understanding to light, and our will to warmth. A garden has light in winter but no warmth, while it has both light and warmth in summer. So when all we have is the light of our understanding, we are like a garden in winter, but when we have both light in our understanding and warmth in our will we are like a garden in summer.

In fact, the wisdom in our understanding comes from spiritual light and the love in our will comes from spiritual warmth, for spiritual light is divine wisdom and spiritual warmth is divine love.

[4] If we fail to turn our backs on evils because they are sins, the cravings of our evils clog the deeper levels of our earthly mind on the side where our will resides and are like a thick veil, like black clouds beneath the spiritual mind, preventing it from opening. However, as soon as we turn our backs on evils because they are sins, the Lord flows in from heaven, takes the veil away, dispels the cloud, and opens the spiritual mind, thereby admitting us to heaven.

[5] As already noted, as long as cravings for evil behavior clog the deeper levels of the earthly mind, we are in hell, but as soon as those cravings are dispelled by the Lord, we are in heaven. Again, as long as cravings for evil behavior clog the deeper levels of the earthly mind we are earthly people, but as soon as those cravings are dispelled by the Lord, we are spiritual people. Again, as long as cravings for evil behavior clog the deeper levels of the earthly mind we are animals, differing from them only in that we are capable of thinking and talking, even about things we cannot see with our eyes (we can do this because of the ability of our understanding to be lifted up into heaven's light). As soon as those cravings have been dispelled by the Lord, though, we are human because we are thinking what is true in our understanding because of what is good in our will. And yet again, as long as cravings for evil behavior clog the deeper levels of the earthly mind we are like a garden in winter, but as soon as those cravings are dispelled by the Lord, we are like a garden in summer.

[6] In the Word, the union of our will and understanding is meant by "heart and soul" and by "heart and spirit," as when it says that we are to love God with all our heart and with all our soul (Matthew 22:37) and that God will give a new heart and a new spirit (Ezekiel 11:19; 36:26, 27).

Our "heart" means our will and its love, while our "soul" or "spirit" means our understanding and its wisdom.

To the Extent That We Turn Our Backs on All Kinds of False Witness Because They Are Sins, We Love Truth

UNDERSTOOD on an earthly level, bearing false witness means not only committing legal perjury but also telling lies and slandering others. Understood on a spiritual level, bearing false witness means saying and convincing ourselves that something false is true and that something evil is good, and the reverse. Understood on the highest level, though, bearing false witness means blaspheming the Lord and the Word. These are the three meanings of false witness.

The information about the threefold meaning of everything in the Word presented in *Teachings on Sacred Scripture* 5, 6, 7, and following may show that these three are united in people who commit perjury, tell lies, and slander.

Since lying and truth are two opposite things, it follows that to the **88** extent that we turn our backs on lying because it is a sin, we love truth.

To the extent that we love truth we want to know it and we find our **89** hearts moved when we find it. That is the only way to arrive at wisdom; and to the extent that we love to do the truth, we take pleasure in the light that contains it.

This is the same as in the case of the commandments already discussed, such as honesty and fairness in those who turn their backs on all kinds of theft, chastity and purity in those who turn their backs on all kinds of adultery, love and caring in those who turn their backs on all kinds of killing, and so on.

People who are caught up in the opposite attitudes, though, know nothing about all this, even though it involves everything that is actually anything.

90   "Truth" is meant by the seed in the field, which the Lord described as follows:

> A sower went out to sow seed. As he was sowing, some seed fell on a much-trodden path, and the birds of heaven devoured it. Some seed fell on stony places, but as soon as it grew up it withered, because it had no root. Some seed fell among thorns, and the thorns grew up with it and choked it. And some seed fell on good ground, and when it grew up it bore abundant fruit. (Luke 8:5–8; Matthew 13:3–8; Mark 4:3–8)

In this parable the sower is the Lord and the seed is his Word and therefore the truth. The seed on the path refers to the way the Word is viewed by people who do not care about truth. The seed in stony places refers to the way the Word is viewed by people who do care about truth, but not for its own sake, and therefore not deeply. The seed among thorns refers to the way the Word is viewed by people who are caught up in cravings for evil behavior, while the seed in good ground is the way the Word is viewed by people who love the truths that come from the Lord and are found in the Word, the people who bear fruit because their doing of those truths comes from him. We are assured of these meanings by the Lord's explanation (Matthew 13:19–23, 37; Mark 4:14–20; Luke 8:11–15).

We can see from this that the truth of the Word cannot take root in people who do not care about truth or in people who love truth superficially but not deeply or in people who are caught up in cravings for evil behavior. However, it can take root in people whose cravings for evil behavior have been dispelled by the Lord. In these the seed can take root—that is, the truth can take root in their spiritual minds (see the close of §86 above).

91   It is generally thought nowadays that being saved is a matter of believing one thing or another that the church teaches, and that being saved is not a matter of obeying the Ten Commandments in particular—not killing, not committing adultery, not stealing, not bearing false witness; and it is said in a wider sense that the focus should not be on deeds but on faith that comes from God. However, to the extent that we are caught up in evils we do not have faith (see §§42–52 above). Consult your reason and you will clearly see that no killer, adulterer, thief, or false witness can have faith while he or she is caught up in such cravings. You will also clearly see that we cannot dispel these cravings in any other way than by our being unwilling to act on them because they are sins—that is, because they are hellish and diabolical. So if people think that being saved is a matter of believing one thing or another that the church teaches, while at the same time they remain people of this kind, they cannot help being foolish. This is according to what the Lord says in Matthew 7:26.

This is how Jeremiah describes this kind of church:

> Stand in the gate of the house of Jehovah and proclaim this word there: "Thus says Jehovah Sabaoth, the God of Israel: 'Make your ways and your deeds good. Do not put your trust in lying words, saying, "The temple of Jehovah, the temple of Jehovah, the temple of Jehovah are these." Are you going to steal, kill, commit adultery, and tell lies under oath, and then come and stand before me in this house that bears my name and say, "We are delivered" when you are doing these abominations? Has this house become a robbers' cave? Indeed, behold, I have seen it,' says Jehovah." (Jeremiah 7:2, 3, 4, 9, 10, 11)

The Only Way
to Abstain from Sinful Evils
So Thoroughly That We Develop
an Inner Aversion to Them
Is to Do Battle against Them

EVERYONE knows on the basis of the Word and teachings drawn **92** from it that from the time we are born our self-centeredness is evil and that this is why we have an inborn compulsion to love evil behavior and to be drawn into it. We are deliberately vengeful, for example; we deliberately cheat, disparage others, and commit adultery; and if we do not think that these behaviors are sins and resist them for that reason, we do them whenever the opportunity presents itself, as long as our reputation or our wealth is not affected.

Then too, we really enjoy doing such things if we have no religion.

Since this self-centeredness is the taproot of the life we lead, we can **93** see what kind of trees we would be if this root were not pulled up and a new root planted. We would be rotten trees that needed to be cut down and thrown into the fire (see Matthew 3:10; 7:19).

This root is not removed and a new one put in its place unless we see that the evils that constitute it are harmful to our souls, and therefore we want to banish them. However, since they are part of our self-centeredness and therefore give us pleasure, we can do this only reluctantly and in the face of opposition, and therefore by doing battle.

94 Everyone undertakes this battle who believes that heaven and hell are real and that heaven is eternal happiness and hell eternal misery, and who believes that we come into hell if we do evil and into heaven if we do good. Whenever we do battle in this way, we are acting from our inner selves and against the compulsions that constitute the root of evil, because when we are fighting against something we are not intending it, and compulsions are intentions.

We can see from this that the only way to dig out the root of evil is by doing battle against it.

95 The more we do battle and thereby set evils to one side, the more what is good replaces them and we look what is evil in the face from the perspective of what is good and see that the evil is hellish and hideous. Since this is how we see it then, we not only abstain from it but develop an aversion to it and eventually loathe it.

96 When we battle against what is evil, we cannot help but fight using what seems to be our own strength, because if we are not using what seems to be our own strength, we are not doing battle. We are standing there like an automaton, seeing nothing and doing nothing, while constantly thinking on the basis of evil and in favor of it, not against it.

However, we need to be quite clear about the fact that it is the Lord alone who is fighting within us against the evils, that it only seems as though we are using our own strength for the battle, and that the Lord wants it to seem like that because if it does not, no battle occurs, so there is no reformation either.

97 This battle is hard only if we have given free rein to our cravings and indulged in them deliberately, or if we have stubbornly rejected the holy principles of the Word and the church. Otherwise, it is not hard. We need only resist evils in our intentions once a week or twice a month and we will notice a change.

98 The Christian church is called "the church militant." It is called that because it fights against the Devil and therefore against evils that come from hell. ("The Devil" is hell.) The inner trials that church people endure are that fight.

There are many passages in the Word about battles against evils, or **99** trials. That is what these words of the Lord are about:

> I say to you, unless a grain of wheat falls into the ground and dies, it remains alone; but if it dies, it produces much fruit. (John 12:24)

Then there is this:

> Those who wish to come with me must deny themselves and take up their cross and follow me. Those who try to save their own life will lose it, but those who lose their life for my sake and the gospel's will save it. (Mark 8:34, 35)

The "cross" means these trials, as it does also in Matthew 10:38; 16:24; Mark 10:21; and Luke 14:27. "Life" means the life we claim as our own, as it does also in Matthew 10:39; 16:25; Luke 9:24; and especially John 12:25. It is also the life of "the flesh," which "is of no benefit at all" (John 6:63). In the Book of Revelation, the Lord spoke to all the churches about battles against evils and victories over them:

> To *the church in Ephesus:* To those who overcome I will give [food] to eat from the tree of life, which is in the midst of the paradise of God. (Revelation 2:7)

> To *the church in Smyrna:* Those who overcome will not be hurt by the second death. (Revelation 2:11)

> To *the church in Pergamum:* To those who overcome I will give the hidden manna to eat; and I will give them a white stone, and on the stone a new name written that no one knows except the one who receives it. (Revelation 2:17)

> To *the church in Thyatira:* To those who overcome and keep my works to the end I will give power over the nations, and give the morning star. (Revelation 2:26, 28)

> To *the church in Sardis:* [Those who overcome will be clothed in white garments, and I will not blot their names from the Book of Life; I will confess their names before my Father and before his angels. (Revelation 3:5)

> To *the church in Philadelphia:*] Those who overcome I will make pillars in the temple of my God, and will write upon them the name of God, the name of the city of God, the New Jerusalem, which is coming down out of heaven from God, and my new name. (Revelation 3:12)

To *the church in Laodicea:* To those who overcome I will grant to sit with me on my throne. (Revelation 3:21)

100 You may find material specifically about these battles or trials in *The New Jerusalem and Its Heavenly Teachings* (published in London in 1758) §§187–201; on their source and nature, see §§196 and 197; on how and when they happen, §198; on the good they accomplish, §199; on the Lord fighting for us, §200; and on the Lord's battles or trials, §201.

We Need to Abstain from Sinful Evils and Fight against Them As Though We Were Doing So on Our Own

101 IT is part of the divine design that we act in freedom and according to reason, because acting in freedom according to reason is acting on our own.

However, these two powers, freedom and reason, are not our own. They are the Lord's within us; and since we are human they are not taken from us, because we cannot be reformed without them. That is, we cannot practice repentance, we cannot fight against evils and as a result bear fruit that is consistent with repentance [Matthew 3:8; Luke 3:8].

So since we are given freedom and reason by the Lord and we act from them, it follows that we are not acting on our own but as though we were on our own.[a]

102 The Lord loves us and wants to dwell with us but cannot love and dwell with us unless he is received and loved in return. This is the one and only means to union. This is why the Lord gives us freedom and the power to reason—the freedom of thinking and intending with seeming autonomy, and the power of reason that serves as our guide. It

---

a. On our being given freedom by the Lord, see §§19 and 20 above and §§589–596 and 597–603 in *Heaven and Hell*. On what freedom is, see *The New Jerusalem and Its Heavenly Teachings* (published in London in 1758) §§141–149.

is impossible to love and be united with someone who is unresponsive, impossible to come in and abide with someone who is unreceptive. It is because our own receptiveness and responsiveness are given by the Lord that the Lord said,

> Abide in me, and I [will abide] in you. (John 15:4)

> Those who abide in me and in whom I abide bear much fruit. (John 15:5)

> On that day you will know that you are in me and I am in you. (John 14:20)

The Lord also tells us that he is present in whatever is true and good that we have received and that is within us:

> If you abide in me and my words abide in you . . . If you keep my commandments, you will abide in my love. (John 15:7, 10)

> The people who love me are those who have my commandments and do them; and I will love them and dwell with them. (John 14:21, 23)

So the Lord dwells with us in what is his own, and we dwell in what the Lord is giving us and are therefore in the Lord.

Since the Lord gives us this ability to respond in turn—and therefore a mutual relationship [with him]—he says that we are to repent, and no one can repent without a sense of autonomy. **103**

> Jesus said, "Unless you repent, you will all perish." (Luke 13:3, 5)

> Jesus said, "The kingdom of God is at hand. Repent, and believe in the gospel." (Mark 1:14, 15)

> Jesus said, "I have come to call sinners to repentance." (Luke 5:32)

> Jesus said to the churches, "Repent!" (Revelation 2:5, 16, 21, 22; 3:3)

> They did not repent of their deeds. (Revelation 16:11)

Since the Lord gives us this ability to respond in turn—and therefore a mutual relationship [with him]—the Lord says that we are to do his commandments and bear fruit: **104**

> Why do you call me, "Lord, Lord," and not do what I say? (Luke 6:46–49)

> If you know these things, you are blessed if you do them. (John 13:17)

> You are my friends if you do what I command you. (John 15:14)

Whoever does and teaches [the commandments] will be called great in the kingdom of the heavens. (Matthew 5:19)

Everyone who hears my words and does them I will liken to a wise man. (Matthew 7:24)

Bear fruit that is consistent with repentance. (Matthew 3:8)

Make the tree good and its fruit good. (Matthew 12:33)

The kingdom will be given to a nation that bears its fruits. (Matthew 21:43)

Every tree that does not bear fruit is cut down and thrown into the fire. (Matthew 7:19)

and often elsewhere.

We can see from these passages that we are to act [not] on our own, but through the power of the Lord, which we must pray for; and that this is acting as if we were on our own.

105 Since the Lord gives us this ability to respond in turn—and therefore a mutual relationship [with him]—we must therefore give an account of our deeds and be recompensed accordingly, for the Lord says:

The Son of Humanity is going to come, and he will repay all people according to their deeds. (Matthew 16:27)

Those who have done what is good will go forth into the resurrection of life, and those who have done what is evil will go forth into the resurrection of condemnation. (John 5:29)

Their works follow them. (Revelation 14:13)

All were judged according to their works. (Revelation 20:13)

Behold, I am coming, and my reward is with me, to give to all according to what they have done. (Revelation 22:12)

If we had no ability to respond, we could not be held accountable.

106 Since it is up to us to be receptive and to respond in turn, the church teaches that we are to examine ourselves, confess our sins in the presence of God, stop committing them, and lead a new life. Every church in the Christian world teaches this, as stated in §§3–8.

107 If we did not have the power to be receptive and therefore had no apparent ability to think independently, faith could not have even entered the discussion, since faith does not come from us either. If it were not for that ability to be receptive, we would be like straw blowing in the wind, and would stand around lifelessly, with our mouths gaping and our hands hanging limp, waiting for something to flow in, neither thinking nor doing anything about what matters for our salvation. We are in no way the active force in these matters, true, but we do react seemingly on our own.

These matters will be presented in still clearer light, though, in the works on angelic wisdom.

If We Turn Our Backs on Evils for Any Other Reason Than That They Are Sins, We Are Not Turning Our Backs on Them but Are Simply Making Sure They Are Not Visible in the Eyes of the World

THERE are moral individuals who keep the commandments of the second tablet of the Ten Commandments, who do not cheat, blaspheme, take vengeance, or commit adultery, and who are convinced that such behavior is evil because it is harmful to the state and therefore contrary to the laws of humanity. They also practice caring, honesty, fairness, and chastity. **108**

If they are doing these good things and turning their backs on evil things only because the latter are evil, though, and not because they are sins as well, these people are merely earthly, and in merely earthly individuals the root of the evil remains in place and is not removed. So the good things they do are not good, because they arise from the doers themselves.

Moral earthly individuals can look just like moral spiritual individuals to people on earth, but not to angels in heaven. To angels in heaven they look like lifeless wooden statues if the individuals are focused on goodness, and like lifeless marble statues if they are focused on truth. It is **109** different for moral spiritual individuals because a moral earthly person is moral on the outside, while a moral spiritual person is moral on the inside, and the outside has no life apart from the inside. Technically speaking, the outside is alive, of course, but it has no life worthy of the name.

110   The compulsions to evil that constitute our deeper nature from birth can be set aside only by the Lord, because the Lord flows from what is spiritual into what is earthly, but of ourselves we flow from what is earthly into what is spiritual. This latter flow goes against the divine design and does not operate on our compulsions and set them aside but envelops them more and more tightly as we reinforce them. So since this means that our inherited evil remains hidden and enclosed within us, when we become spirits after death it bursts the coverings that veiled it on earth and breaks out like pus from an ulcer that has been healed only superficially.

111   The reasons we may be moral in outward form are many and varied, but if we are not inwardly moral as well, we are not really moral at all. For example, we may refrain from adultery and fornication out of fear of civil law and its penalties, fear of loss of our good name and therefore our rank, fear of associated diseases, fear of being berated by a wife at home and a consequent loss of tranquillity, fear of vengeance by a husband or relatives. We may refrain because of poverty or greed, because of incompetence caused by disease, abuse, age, or impotence—in fact, if we refrain from them because of any earthly or moral law and not because of spiritual law as well, we are adulterers and lechers all the same. That is, we believe that they are not sins and in our spirits regard them as not illegal in the sight of God. This means that in spirit we are committing them even though we are not doing so in the flesh in this world; so when we become spirits after death, we speak openly in favor of them.

We can see from this that irreligious people can turn their backs on evils as harmful, but only Christians can turn their backs on evils because they are sins.

112   It is much the same with all kinds of theft and cheating, all kinds of killing and vengeance, all kinds of false witness and lying. None of us can be cleansed and purified from them by our own strength. There are infinite complexities hidden within a compulsion that we see as a single, simple thing, but the Lord sees the tiniest details in complete sequence.

In a word, we cannot regenerate ourselves. That is, we cannot form a new heart and a new spirit within ourselves [Ezekiel 11:19; 36:26]. Only the Lord, who is the true Reformer and Regenerator, can do this; so if we try to make ourselves new with our own plans and our own intelligence, this is like putting rouge on a disfigured face or smearing cleansing cream over an area that is inwardly infected.

That is why the Lord says in Matthew,

113

> Blind Pharisee, cleanse the inside of the cup and the plate first, so that the outside of them may be clean as well. (Matthew 23:26)

and in Isaiah,

> Wash yourselves! Purify yourselves! Take away the evil of your deeds from *before my eyes!* Stop doing evil! And then, even if your sins have been like scarlet, they will become white like snow; even if they have been as red as purple-dyed cloth, they will be like wool. (Isaiah 1:16, 18)

*   *   *   *   *   *

The following should be appended to what has now been said: first, for us all, Christian charity is actually a matter of faithfully performing a useful occupation. If we turn our backs on evils because they are sins, we are daily doing what is good, and are ourselves the useful functions we should be in the body politic. This means that the larger body is being cared for, and so is each member in particular. Second, all the other things we do [outside of our occupation] are not works of charity, strictly speaking, but are either further reflections of our charity, or else simply good deeds or things we are properly obligated to do.

114

Teachings
for the
New Jerusalem
on
Faith

Teachings for the New Jerusalem on Faith

Faith Is an Inner Recognition of Truth

NOWADAYS, people understand "faith" to mean nothing more than thinking that something is true because the church teaches it and because it is not obvious to the intellect. In fact, the common saying is, "Believe, and don't doubt." If someone replies, "I don't understand it," people say, "That's why you have to believe it." The result is that today's faith is faith in the unknown and can be called "blind faith"; and since it involves a decree from one person to another, it is faith handed down from the past.

It will become clear in the following pages that this is not a spiritual faith.

Real faith is simply recognizing that something is so because it is true. This means that people who are devoted to real faith both think and say, "This is true, and that's why I believe it." That is, faith is dependent on truth, and what is true is the object of faith. So if we do not understand that something is true, we say, "I don't know whether this is true or not, so I don't believe it yet. How can I believe something that doesn't make sense to me? It may be false."

3   All the same, the widely shared opinion is that no one can understand things that are spiritual or theological because they are supernatural. However, spiritual truths can be grasped just as earthly ones are—perhaps not as clearly, but still, when we hear them we do get a sense as to whether they are true or not. This is especially so in the case of people who have a longing for truth.

I have been taught this by an abundance of experience. I have been granted the opportunity to talk with people who lacked education, people who lacked common sense, and people who lacked intelligence, and with people who, despite having been born in the church and having therefore heard something about the Lord, faith, and caring, were convinced of false ideas or were immersed in evil. I have been granted the opportunity to tell them secrets of wisdom, and they understood and acknowledged everything. At such times, of course, they were in that light of understanding that is common to us all, and also in a state of glory because they were in a condition of understanding. This happened during my interactions with spirits.

These experiences convinced many who were with me that spiritual matters are just as comprehensible as earthly matters—at least when people hear or read them—but hard to understand when people are left on their own to think for themselves. The reason we can understand spiritual matters is that we can be lifted mentally into heaven's light, the light in which all the things we see are spiritual—all the truths that belong to the faith. The light of heaven is spiritual light.

4   This is why the people who have an inner recognition of what is true are those who have a spiritual love for truth. Since angels have this love, they flatly reject the dogma that our intellect must be subject to faith. On the contrary, they say, "Is there any such thing as believing something without first seeing whether it is true?" And if someone says that we must nevertheless believe, they reply, "Do you think you are God, that I should believe you, or that I am so crazy that I will believe some statement in which I see nothing true? Make me see it." Then the adherent of dogmatism slinks away.

The angels' wisdom consists entirely in seeing and understanding the things they are thinking about.

5   There is a spiritual perspective, of which few people know anything at all, a perspective that inflows in the case of people who have a longing for truth and tells them inwardly whether what they are hearing or reading is true or not. When we are reading the Word with enlightenment from the Lord, we have this perspective. Having enlightenment is nothing more nor less than having a perception and therefore an inner acknowledgment that this or that statement is true. Isaiah calls such people "taught by Jehovah" (Isaiah 54:13; see also John 6:45); and Jeremiah says of them,

> Behold, the days are coming in which I will make a new covenant. This will be the covenant: I will put my law in their midst and I will write it on their heart. No longer will people teach their friends or their family, saying, "Know Jehovah," for they will all know me. (Jeremiah 31:31, 33, 34)

We can see from all this that faith and truth are one and the same; **6** and this is why the ancients, who thought more about truths than we do because they had a longing for them, talked about "truth" rather than "faith." This is also why in Hebrew the same word—for example, *emuna,* and also *amen*—can mean both "truth" and "faith."

The reason the Lord talked about faith in the Gospels and Revelation **7** was that the Jews did not believe it was true that he was the Messiah foretold by the prophets; and wherever the truth is not believed, faith enters the discussion. Nevertheless, it is one thing to have faith and believe in the Lord and something else to have faith and believe someone else. We will get to that difference later.

With the regime of the papacy, faith apart from truth entered—even **8** invaded—the church, because the primary bulwark of that religion was ignorance of the truth. That is why the reading of the Word was forbidden—otherwise people could not have been worshiped as having divine authority, and there could have been no invocation of saints, and no wholesale introduction of idolatrous practices—like the belief that cadavers and bones and their tombs are holy (and therefore profitable). We can see from this what monstrous misconceptions blind faith can produce.

Blind faith also lived on among many Protestants because they separated faith from caring; and if people separate these two things, then they **9** cannot help but be ignorant of what is true, and they define faith as thinking that something is true apart from any inner recognition that it is true. For such people, ignorance is the defender of dogmatism, because as long as ignorance holds sway, accompanied by the conviction that theological matters are beyond reach, they can say anything and not be contradicted. They can believe that what they say is true and that they understand it.

The Lord said to Thomas, **10**

> Because you have seen me, Thomas, you have believed. Blessed are those who do not see, and yet they believe. (John 20:29)

This does not mean faith apart from an inner recognition of truth, but that people are blessed who do not see the Lord with their eyes as Thomas did and who still believe that he exists, because this recognition occurs in the light of truth from the Word.

11   Since faith is an inner recognition that something is true, and since faith and truth are one and the same (as noted in §§2, 4, 5, and 6 above), it follows that an outward recognition without an inner one is not faith, and that being convinced of something false is not faith.

An outer recognition apart from an inner one is faith in the unknown, and faith in the unknown is nothing but information held in our memory that becomes a conviction if there are arguments to support it. People who hold to such convictions think something is true because someone else has said so, or believe it is true because they have convinced themselves; yet it is as easy to convince ourselves of something false as it is of something true, and sometimes such a conviction is even stronger.

Thinking something is true because we have convinced ourselves of it means thinking what someone else has said is true and looking for support for it without first examining it for ourselves.

12   Some may think to themselves or say to someone else, "Who is capable of having the inner recognition of truth that is faith? Not I." I will tell them how they can: Turn your back on evils because they are sins and turn to the Lord, and you will have as much of that inner recognition as you wish.

You may see in *Teachings about Life for the New Jerusalem* 18–31 that if we turn our backs on evils because they are sins we are in the Lord; in §§32–41 that we then love what is true and see it; and in §§42–52 that we then have faith.

The "Inner Recognition of Truth" That Is Faith Is Found Only in People Who Are Devoted to Caring

13   HAVING just said what faith is, I need now to say what caring is. Caring originates in a desire to do something good. Since what is good loves what is true, this desire leads to a desire for truth and therefore to the recognition of what is true, which is faith. By these steps, in proper sequence, a desire to do something good takes form and turns into caring. This is how caring develops from its origin, which is a desire to do something good, through faith, which is a recognition of what is true, to its goal, which is caring. The goal is the doing of something.

We can see from this how love, which is a desire to do something good, brings forth faith, which is the same as recognizing what is true, and by this means brings forth caring, which is the same as love acting through faith.

To put it more clearly, a thing that is good must be of use, so the origin of caring is wanting to be of use; and since usefulness loves the means [of being of use], it prompts a desire for those means and leads to a recognition of them. So by the steps in this sequence, wanting to be of use takes visible form and becomes caring.

14

This sequence is like the sequence of everything that starts in our will and moves through our understanding into the actions of our bodies. Our will accomplishes nothing on its own apart from our understanding, nor does our understanding on its own apart from our will. They need to act together for anything to happen.

15

That is to say, a motivating feeling, which comes from our will, has no effect on its own except by means of thought, which is an activity of our faculty of understanding; and the converse holds true as well. They must act together for anything to happen.

Think it through. If you empty thinking of any feeling that comes from some love, can you think? Or by the same token, if you deprive a motivating feeling of its thought, can you accomplish anything? Or again, if you empty thought of its motivating feeling, can you talk, or if you deprive a motivating feeling of its thinking or understanding, can you do anything?

That is how it is with caring and faith.

Comparison with a tree may serve to illustrate this. In its first origin, a tree is a seed in which there is a drive to produce fruit. Stimulated by warmth, this drive first produces roots, and then from the roots a shoot or stem with branches, leaves, and finally fruit. That is how the drive to produce fruit manifests itself. We can see from this that the drive to produce fruit is constant throughout the whole process until it becomes manifest, since if it were to fail, the power to grow would promptly die.

16

This is how the illustration works: The tree is the person. Our drive to produce the means to an end comes from our will and passes into our understanding. Our shoot or stem and its branches and leaves are the means we use, means called the truths that belong to religious faith. The fruits, which in the case of the tree are the final effects of its drive to be fruitful, are in our case the useful acts in which our will becomes manifest.

We can see from this that our will to be of service by using our understanding is constant throughout the whole process until finally it becomes manifest.

On will and understanding and their union, see *Teachings about Life for the New Jerusalem* 43.

17 We can see from what has now been said that caring, to the extent that it is a prompting to do something good, something of use, brings forth faith as its means, through which it becomes manifest. This means that to bring forth something of use, caring and faith must act together.

It also means that faith does not accomplish anything good or useful by itself, but only from caring as its source. Faith, in fact, is just caring in its middle phase, so it is a fallacy to think that faith brings forth what is good the way a tree brings forth fruit. The tree is not faith; the tree is the person.

18 It is important to know that caring and faith are united in the same way that our will and our understanding are united, since our will is the part of us that cares and our understanding is the part of us that has faith. It is also important to know that caring and faith are united in the same way our desiring and our thinking are united, since our will is the part of us that feels desire and our understanding is the part of us that thinks. And again, caring and faith are united in the same way that goodness and truth are united, since what is good is the object of the desire in our will and what is true is the object of the thinking in our understanding.

[2] In short, caring and faith are united in the same way that essence and form are united, because the essence of faith is caring and the form of caring is faith. So we can see that faith without caring is like a form with no essence, which is nothing, and that caring without faith is like an essence with no form, which also is nothing.

19 Our caring and faith work exactly the same way as the motion of the heart that we call systole and diastole and the motion of the lungs that we call breathing. There is also a complete correspondence between these two motions and our will and understanding and therefore also our caring and faith, which is why will and its motivating feelings are meant by "the heart" in the Word, and understanding and its thinking by "the breath" in the Word and also by "the spirit." So "breathing one's last" is no longer living and "giving up the ghost" is no longer breathing.

[2] It follows, then, that there can be no faith without caring or caring without faith, and that faith without caring is like the breathing of the lungs without a heart. This is impossible for any living creature; only an automaton could do it. Caring without faith is like having a heart but no lungs, in which case we would have no awareness that we were alive. So caring does useful things by means of faith the way the heart accomplishes action by means of the lungs.

The likeness between "heart" and caring on the one hand and "lungs" and faith on the other is so strong that in the spiritual world everyone can tell simply from people's breathing what their faith is like and from their heartbeat what their caring is like. Angels and spirits live by heartbeat and breathing just as we do, which is why they feel, think, act, and talk as we do in the world.

Since caring is love for our neighbor, I need to say what "our neighbor" is. In an earthly sense, our neighbor is humankind both collectively and individually. Humankind collectively understood is the church, the country, and the community; humankind individually understood is the fellow citizen who in the Word is called our brother or sister or companion.   **20**

In a spiritual sense, though, our neighbor is whatever is good, and since useful service is good, useful service is our neighbor in a spiritual sense.

It is important for everyone to realize that spiritually speaking, useful service is our neighbor. Who actually loves someone simply as "someone"? No, we love people because of what is within them, what makes them the kind of people they are. That is, we love them for their nature, because that is what each human being is. The quality we love is their usefulness and is what we call "good"; so this is our neighbor.

Since the Word is spiritual at heart, this is the spiritual meaning of "loving our neighbor."

It is one thing, though, when we love our neighbors for the benefit or service they offer us and another thing to love them for the benefit or service we offer them. Even when we are evil we can love our neighbors   **21** for the benefit or service they offer us, but only when we are good can we love our neighbors for the benefit or service we offer them. Then we are loving to do good because it is good—loving useful service because we have a desire to be of use. The difference between the two attitudes is described by the Lord in Matthew 5:43–47.

People often say, "I love such-and-such a person because that person loves me and does me good," but loving others for this reason alone is not loving them deeply, unless we ourselves are intent on what is good and love the good things that they do for that reason. That is being devoted to caring: the other is being focused on a kind of friendship that is not the same as caring.

When we love others because we care about them, we unite with the good they do and not with their personality, except insofar and as long as they are engaged in doing what is good. Then we are spiritual and are loving our neighbor spiritually. If we love others merely out of friendship, though, we unite ourselves with their personality, including the evil that belongs to them. In that case it is hard for us to separate ourselves after death from a personality that is devoted to evil, though in the former case, we can.

Caring makes this distinction by means of faith because faith is truth, and when through truth we are truly caring we look carefully and see what we should love; and when we are loving and benefiting others, we focus on the quality of usefulness in what we are doing.

22   Love for the Lord is what "love" really means, and love for our neighbor is caring. There can be no love for the Lord in us except when we are caring: it is in this that the Lord unites with us.

Since faith in its essence is caring, it follows that no one can have faith in the Lord except while caring. Union comes from caring, through faith—a union of the Lord with us through caring and a union of us with the Lord through faith. On the reciprocal nature of this union, see *Teachings about Life for the New Jerusalem* 102–107.

23   To summarize, to the extent that we turn our backs on evils because they are sins and turn to the Lord, we are engaged in caring, and therefore in faith to the same extent.

On our being engaged in caring to the extent that we turn our backs on evils because they are sins and turn toward the Lord, see *Teachings about Life for the New Jerusalem* 67–73 and 74–91, and on our having faith to the same extent see §§42–52. On the true meaning of the word "caring," see §114 of that work.

We may conclude from all this that a saving faith, the faith that is an inner recognition of what is true, can be found only in people who are caring. **24**

Our Knowledge of What Is True and Good Does Not Become Faith until We Are Engaged in Caring. Once We Have a Faith That Is Born of Caring, Though, That Knowledge Becomes a Resource That Gives Form to Our Faith

RIGHT from earliest childhood we are eager to know things. Because of this we learn a great many things, some of which will be useful to us and some of which will not. When we grow up, we get involved in some occupation and absorb information about it; and as we do, the occupation becomes a way for us to be useful, and we begin to love it. This is how our love of being useful begins; and this love leads us to also love the means that allow us to do our occupation and make it effective. **25**

This process applies to everyone in this world because we all have some occupation to which we progress, beginning from the service we envision as a goal, through the means, to the actual service that is the result. However, since this service and its means have to do with life in this world, loving it is an earthly type of love.

Since we all not only look toward what is useful for our lives in this world but should also look toward what is useful for our lives in heaven (after all, we will get there after life in this world, and that is where we will go on living forever), from our childhood we acquire some familiarity with what is good and true from the Word, from the teachings of the church, or from sermons, and this knowledge is relevant to our eternal life. We store this away in our earthly memory, in greater or lesser abundance **26** depending on our own desire to know, a desire that is both inborn and reinforced by various stimuli.

27 All this knowledge, though, no matter how much or how valuable, is nothing more than a resource out of which a caring faith can be formed; and this kind of faith is formed only as we turn our backs on evils because they are sins.

If we turn our backs on evils because they are sins, then this knowledge becomes part of our faith, which has some spiritual life in it; but if we do not turn our backs on evils because they are sins, then our knowledge is nothing but knowledge, and does not become part of a faith that has spiritual life within it.

28 This resource is of critical importance because without it no faith can take form. Our knowledge of what is true and good becomes part of our faith and strengthens it. If we have no such knowledge, faith does not happen. There is no such thing as an empty faith, a faith without content. If we have only a little of such knowledge, our faith is weak and needy. If we have an abundance of such knowledge, our faith becomes rich and full in proportion to that abundance.

29 It is important to know, though, that faith is supported by knowledge of what is *genuinely* true and good; this is definitely not the case with knowledge of what is false. Faith is truth (see §§5–11 above), and since falsity contradicts truth, it destroys faith. Caring, too, cannot occur where there are nothing but falsities, since as noted in §18 above, caring and faith are united the way goodness and truth are united.

It also follows from all this that a total absence of knowledge of what is true and good makes for no faith; slight knowledge makes for some faith; and an abundance of knowledge makes for a faith that is enlightened in proportion to its fullness.

The quality of faith we have as a result of caring determines the quality of our intelligence.

30 There are many people, too, who do not have an inner recognition of what is true but still have a faith that comes from caring. These are people who have turned toward the Lord in their lives and who have refrained from evil behavior for religious reasons, but who have been hindered from thinking about truths by worldly concerns and by their professional responsibilities as well as by a lack of truth on the part of their teachers. More deeply, or in spirit, though, they are able to recognize what is true, because they are drawn to it; so after they die, become spirits, and are taught by angels, they recognize what is true and are overjoyed to receive it.

However, it is different for people who have not turned toward the Lord in their lives and have failed to refrain from evil behavior in accord with their religion. Inwardly or in spirit they do not feel drawn to truth and therefore have no ability to recognize it. So when they become spirits after death and are taught by angels, they are unwilling to acknowledge what is true and therefore do not accept it. Inside an evil life there is a hatred of truth, while inside a good life there is a love for truth.

The knowledge of what is true and good that we have before we have **31** faith might be seen by some people as constituting faith, but in actuality it is not faith. Our thinking and saying we believe does not mean that we actually do believe, or that we have faith—it is just that we think we do. The things we know do not spring from an inner recognition that they are truths; and a faith that things are true when we do not actually know whether they are or not is a kind of bias quite remote from any inner acknowledgment. However, as soon as caring takes root, this knowledge becomes part of our faith—though only to the extent that there is caring within it.

In the first stage, before there is a sense of caring, it seems to us that faith is primary and caring secondary. In the second stage, though, when there is a sense of caring, faith becomes secondary and caring primary. The first stage is called "reformation" and the second is called "regeneration." When we are in this latter stage, day by day our wisdom grows, and day by day goodness causes our truths to multiply and bear fruit. Then we are like a tree that is bearing fruit and developing seeds in the fruit that will yield new trees and eventually an orchard.

Then we become truly human, and after death we will be angels, whose life is an embodiment of caring and whose form is an embodiment of faith. That form will be as beautiful as our faith. But our faith will no longer be called faith: it will be called an understanding.

This shows us that every bit of faith comes from caring and nothing from faith itself. It also shows us that caring produces faith, but faith does not produce caring. The knowledge of truth that comes first is like grain stored in a cellar, which does not nourish us at all until we want to make some food with it and we take some out.

I need to tell also how faith is formed out of caring. Each of us has an **32** earthly mind and a spiritual mind, the earthly mind for this world and the spiritual mind for heaven. We have access to both with respect to our intellect but not with respect to our will, until we turn our backs on evils and reject them because they are sins. When we do this, our spiritual mind is opened with respect to our will as well, and a spiritual warmth from heaven flows into our earthly mind. Essentially, this warmth is caring, and it brings to life our knowledge of what is true and good, a knowledge that is in our earthly mind, and forms a faith out of it. Again, this is like a tree that does not get any vegetative life until warmth from the sun flows into it and unites itself with light, as happens in spring.

There is actually a complete parallel between humans coming to life and the sprouting of a tree. The parallel rests on the fact that earthly warmth causes the latter and heavenly warmth causes the former. That is why the Lord so often compared people to trees.

33   These few thoughts may suffice to show that our knowledge of what is true and good does not constitute faith until we are committed to caring, but that it is a resource from which a caring faith can be formed.

Our knowledge of what is true is true for us when we have been regenerated. So is our knowledge of what is good, since our learning about what is good takes place in our understanding, but a desire to do what is good develops in our will. So we call something true if it is in our understanding and call it good if it is in our will.

The [True] Christian Faith
in One All-Encompassing View

34   THE following is the [true] Christian faith in one all-encompassing view:

The Lord from eternity, who is Jehovah, came into the world to gain control over the hells and to glorify his human nature. Without this no human being could have been saved; and those are saved who believe in him.

35   I refer to this belief as the faith in one all-encompassing view because it is inherent in the faith, and what is inherent in the faith must be present throughout it and in every detail of it.

Inherent in this faith is the belief that God, in whom there is a trinity, is one in person and in essence, and that the Lord is God.

Inherent in this faith is the belief that no human being could have been saved if the Lord had not come into the world.

Inherent in this faith is the belief that the Lord came into the world to move hell away from us and that he moved it away by means of battles against it and victories over it. That is how he gained control over it, brought it back into order, and made it obey him.

Also inherent in this faith is the belief that the Lord came into the world to glorify the human nature that he took on in the world—that is, to unite it to the divine nature that was its source. Once he had gained control over hell, this allowed him to keep it in order and obedient to him forever. Since neither of these goals could have been achieved without trials, even to the absolute extreme, and since the absolute extreme was his suffering on the cross, he underwent this.

These are beliefs concerning the Lord that are central to the [true] Christian faith.

Central to the [true] Christian faith as it applies to us is that we believe in the Lord, since believing in him is the union with him that gives us salvation. Believing in him is trusting that he saves people; and since we can have this trust only if we live good lives, believing in him also means leading a good life. **36**

I have elsewhere dealt specifically with these two central elements of the [true] Christian faith: with the *first,* the one about the Lord, in *Teachings for the New Jerusalem on the Lord,* and with the *second,* the one that focuses on us, in *Teachings about Life for the New Jerusalem;* so there is no need to expand them further here. **37**

The Present-Day Faith
in One All-Encompassing View

THE following is the present-day faith in one all-encompassing view: **38**

God the Father sent his Son to pay for the sins of the human race; because of this merit on the part of the Son, the Father feels compassion

and saves those who believe this. (Others would say, "Who believe this
and also do what is good.")

39 To make the nature of this faith clearer, I would like to add a list of
things that it claims to be the case.

1. The present-day faith claims that God the Father and God the Son
   are two, both of whom have existed from eternity.

2. It claims that God the Son came into the world, as a result of the will
   of the Father, to pay for the sins of the human race, which otherwise
   would have perished in eternal death because of divine justice, which
   [those who hold to these beliefs] also call retributive justice.

3. It claims that the Son paid for our sins by his fulfillment of the law
   and by his suffering on the cross.

4. It claims that the Father gave mercy because the Son did these things.

5. It claims that the Son's merit is credited to those who believe this.

6. It claims that this crediting of merit happens instantaneously and
   therefore, if it has not happened before, it can happen at the last
   hour of death.

7. It claims that [when it happens], some element of trial occurs, fol-
   lowed by a liberation by means of this faith.

8. It claims that those [who have this faith] gain a special assurance and
   confidence.

9. It claims that justification is granted especially to these individuals,
   with the full grace of the Father for the sake of the Son, as well as
   forgiveness of all their sins, and therefore salvation.

10. The more learned claim that there is a striving for goodness in these
    people that works very subtly but does not openly direct their will.
    Others claim that this works openly. In either case, the Holy Spirit
    is the agent.

11. Most people, though, who have convinced themselves that we are
    incapable of doing anything that is genuinely good on our own with-
    out claiming credit for it and that we are not under the yoke of the law,
    leave all this out and give no thought to whether the life they are living
    is good or evil. They say to themselves that doing good does not save
    and doing evil does not damn, because faith alone does everything.

12. For the most part, they claim that their understanding must be sub-
    ordinated to this faith. For them, "faith" means anything they do
    not understand.

40 I will forego a detailed examination and evaluation of whether their
claims are the truth. The truth is quite clear from what has already been

said, and especially from the material from the Word presented and supported with reasoning in *Teachings for the New Jerusalem on the Lord* and *Teachings about Life for the New Jerusalem.*

All the same, to show the nature of a faith divorced from caring and a faith not divorced from it, I would like to share something I heard from one of heaven's angels. This angel described having talked with many Protestants to learn about their faith, and told of a conversation with one devoted to a faith divorced from caring and a conversation with one devoted to a faith not divorced from caring. The angel told me what questions had been posed and what the responses had been; and since they can shed light on the subject, I would now like to present these conversations. **41**

The angel told me of the following conversation with the individual who was devoted to a faith divorced from caring. **42**

"Friend, who are you?"

"I am a Protestant Christian."

"What is your theology, and what religious practice does it lead to?"

"Faith."

"What is your faith?"

"My faith is that *God the Father sent his Son to make complete amends for the human race, and that those who believe this are saved.*"

"What else do you know about salvation?"

"Salvation is granted through this faith alone."

"What do you know about redemption?"

"Redemption was effected through the suffering on the cross; the merit of the Son is credited to us through this faith."

"What do you know about regeneration?"

"Regeneration happens by means of this faith."

"What do you know about repentance and the forgiveness of sins?"

"They happen by means of this faith."

"Tell me what you know about love and caring."

"They are this faith."

"Tell me what you know about good works."

"They are this faith."

"Tell me what you think of all the commandments in the Word."

"They are in this faith."

"So you do not do anything?"

"What should I do? On my own, I cannot do anything good that is really good."

"Can you have faith on your own?"

"I cannot."

"Then how can you have faith?"

"I don't ask questions about this; I just have to have faith."

Finally, "Do you know anything else, anything at all, about salvation?"

"What else is there to know, when salvation is granted through this faith alone?"

But then the angel said, "You sound like someone who keeps playing the same note on a flute. All I hear is 'faith.' If that is all you know, and nothing else, then you don't know anything. Go see your companions." So the Protestant Christian went and met others in a wilderness where there was no grass. When the angels were asked why there was not even grass there, they said, "Because they have no trace of a church."

43 The following is the conversation of the angel with the individual who was devoted to a faith not divorced from caring.

"Friend, who are you?"

"I am a Protestant Christian."

"What is your theology, and what religious practice does it lead to?"

"Faith and caring."

"That is two things."

"They cannot be separated."

"What is faith?"

"Believing what the Word teaches us."

"What is caring?"

"Doing what the Word teaches."

"Do you just believe this, or do you also do it?"

"I do it as well."

The angel from heaven then looked at this individual and said, "My friend, come with me and live with us."

The Nature of a Faith Divorced from Caring

44 TO show what faith divorced from caring is really like, I need to present it stark naked. This is how it looks.

> God the Father, outraged by the human race, rejected it from himself and for reasons of justice decided to get even by damning it forever.

Then he said to the Son, "Go down, fulfill the law, and take upon your-self the damnation assigned to them. Then perhaps I will have mercy." So the Son went down, fulfilled the law, and allowed himself to be hung on the cross and brutally murdered. Once this had happened, he went back to the Father and said, interceding for them, "I have taken upon myself the damnation of the human race; now be merciful to them." The Father answered, though, "I cannot do it for their sakes, but since I saw you on the cross and then saw your blood, I have become merciful. Still, I will not pardon them, but I will credit them with your merit, but only for the people who acknowledge what you have done. This must be the faith through which they can be saved."

This is that faith in stark naked form. Can anyone whose reason is at all enlightened fail to see in it absurd notions that run counter to the divine essence itself? For example, there is the notion that a God who is love itself and mercy itself could be moved by rage and vengefulness to damn us and consign us to hell. There is the notion that God chose to be moved to mercy by transferring the damnation to his Son and by gazing at his suffering on the cross and his blood. **45**

Can anyone whose reason is at all enlightened fail to see that no God worthy of the name could say, "I do not pardon them, but I am transfer-ring your merit to them"? Or even, "Now let them live as they wish and they will be saved as long as they believe this"? And so on.

The reason this has not been seen, though, is that they have per-suaded people that faith is blind and have used this notion to close peo-ple's eyes and plug their ears. **46**

Close people's eyes and plug their ears—that is, prevent them from thinking with any understanding—and people who have some notion of eternal life will believe anything you say, even if you say that God can be angry and breathe vengeance, that God can inflict eternal damnation on anyone, that God chooses to be moved to mercy by the blood of his Son and transfer this as credit to our accounts as though it were ours and save us simply by what we think. People will believe, for example, that one God could make a deal with another God (of the same essence) and lay down requirements, and things of that sort.

Open your own eyes, though, and unplug your ears—that is, think intelligently about these matters—and you will see how they clash with the actual truth.

Close people's eyes and plug their ears—that is, prevent them from thinking with any understanding—and can't you then induce a belief **47** that God has given all his power to some person to act as God on earth? Can't you induce a belief that we are to pray to dead people, that we are to bare our heads and bend our knees to their images, to regard their corpses, their bones, and their tombs as holy and worthy of reverence?

But if you open your own eyes and unplug your ears, that is, if you think about these matters with some understanding, will you not see these beliefs as monstrous things that are appalling to human reason?

48 When people whose understanding has been closed because of their religion accept these and similar beliefs, can't we compare the church in which they worship to a cave or underground grotto where they do not know what they are seeing? And can't we compare their religion to living in a house without windows and the voice of their worship to noise rather than speech?

Heaven's angels cannot talk with people like this because neither side understands the language of the other.

The Philistines Mentioned in the Word Represent People Devoted to a Faith Divorced from Caring

49 IN the Word all the names of nations and peoples as well as of persons and places are used to mean matters of the church. The church itself is meant by Israel and Judah because that is where it was established; and various other religious perspectives are meant by the surrounding nations and peoples—compatible perspectives by the good nations and incompatible ones by the evil nations.

There are two evil versions of religion into which all churches degenerate with the passage of time. One is the corruption of what a given church has that is good and the other is the distortion of what that church has that is true. The origin of the version that pollutes the good qualities of the church is the love of having complete control [over others], and the origin of the second version, which distorts the true ideas of the church, is pride in our own intelligence.

The version that comes from a love of having complete control is the one meant in the Word by Babylon, and the version that comes from pride in our own intelligence is the one meant in the Word by Philistia.

Everyone knows who the Babylonians are in our own times, but not who the Philistines are. The Philistines are people who are devoted to faith but not to caring.

From various things that the Word, when spiritually understood, tells us about the Philistines, we can determine that they are those who are devoted to faith but not to caring. This we can tell both from their arguments with the servants of Abraham and Isaac in Genesis 21 and 26 and from their wars with the children of Israel in Judges, Samuel, and Kings. In fact, all the wars described in the Word have a spiritual meaning; they reflect and symbolize spiritual wars. And since this form of religion, which is one of faith divorced from caring, is constantly trying to invade the church, the Philistines remained in the land of Canaan and often attacked the children of Israel. **50**

Since the Philistines represented people devoted to a faith divorced from caring, they were called "uncircumcised," and "uncircumcised" means lacking in spiritual love and therefore having only earthly love. Spiritual love is caring. **51**

The reason they were called uncircumcised is that "the circumcised" means those who are devoted to spiritual love. On the Philistines being called "the uncircumcised," see 1 Samuel 17:26, 36; 2 Samuel 1:20; and elsewhere.

We can determine that people devoted to a faith divorced from caring were represented by the Philistines not only from their wars with the children of Israel but also from a number of other things we are told about them in the Word. For example, there is what it says about their idol, Dagon; about the hemorrhoids they were afflicted with and the rats they were invaded by because they had put the ark in their idol's shrine; and about what happened after that (see chapters 5 and 6 of 1 Samuel). There is also Goliath, the Philistine killed by David (see 1 Samuel 17). **52**

As for their idol Dagon, it looked human from the waist up but looked like a fish from the waist down. This was an image of their religion, which seemed to be spiritual because of its faith but was merely earthly because of its lack of caring. The hemorrhoids that afflicted them symbolized their unclean loves; the rats that invaded them symbolized the destruction of the church through its distortions of truth; and Goliath, [the Philistine] killed by David, represented their pride in their own intelligence.

53 We can also see from what the Word's prophets say about the Philistines that they represented people devoted to a faith divorced from caring. There is the following passage from Jeremiah, for example:

> Against the Philistines: Behold, waters are rising up from the north that will become an overflowing river and will flood the earth and all that is in it, the city and all those who live in it. People will cry out and everyone who lives on the earth will wail. Jehovah will devastate the Philistines. (Jeremiah 47:1, 2, 4)

The waters rising up from the north are falsities from hell; their becoming an overflowing river and flooding the earth and all that is in it means the consequent destruction of everything in the church; their flooding the city and all those who live in it means the complete destruction of its teachings; people crying out and everyone who lives on earth wailing means the loss of everything true and good in the church; and Jehovah devastating the Philistines means their demise. From Isaiah:

> All Philistia, do not rejoice because the rod that was striking you has been broken, for out of the root of the serpent will come a basilisk, and its fruit will be a flying fiery serpent. (Isaiah 14:29)

The command to all Philistia not to rejoice means that people devoted to faith divorced from caring should not rejoice in the fact that they are surviving; "for out of the root of the serpent will come a basilisk" means the destruction of everything true they have because of their pride in their own intelligence; "its fruit will be a flying fiery serpent" means rationalizations based on malevolent distortions that oppose what is true and good in the church.

54 We can see from the following passages that circumcision represented purification from evils that are caused by strictly earthly love:

> Circumcise your heart and take away the foreskin of your heart, so that my wrath will not break forth because of the ill will of your deeds. (Jeremiah 4:4)

> Circumcise the foreskin of your heart and no longer stiffen your neck. (Deuteronomy 10:16)

To circumcise the heart or the foreskin of the heart is to purify ourselves from evils.

Conversely, then, being uncircumcised or having a foreskin refers to people who have not been purified from evils caused by strictly earthly love and who are therefore not devoted to caring, and since having a foreskin means being unclean at heart, it says that no one who is uncircumcised at heart or uncircumcised in the flesh is to enter the sanctuary (Ezekiel 44:9); that no uncircumcised person is to eat the Passover meal (Exodus 12:48); and that the uncircumcised are damned (Ezekiel 28:10; 31:18; 32:19).

The Dragon Mentioned in the Book of Revelation Symbolizes People Devoted to a Faith Divorced from Caring

I noted earlier [§49] that in the course of time every church degenerates into two common evil versions of religion, one that comes from a love of having control and one that comes from intellectual pride. I noted that in the Word the first kind of religion is identified and depicted as *Babylon* and the second as *Philistia*.

Now, since the Book of Revelation deals with the state of the Christian church, especially at its close, it deals in general and in particular with these two evil versions of religion. The kind of religion meant by Babylon is described in chapters 17, 18, and 19 as the whore who sat on the scarlet beast, and the kind of religion meant by Philistia is described in chapters 12 and 13 as the dragon, and also as the beast rising up out of the sea and the beast rising up out of the earth.

Until now there has been no way to know that this kind of religion was meant by the dragon and his two beasts. This is because the spiritual meaning of the Word had not yet been opened, so the Book of Revelation had not been understood, and particularly because in the Christian world a form of religion based on faith divorced from caring had become so strong that no one was able to see this. Every evil kind of religion blinds the eyes.

As for the fact that a religion of faith divorced from caring is meant and described in the Book of Revelation by the dragon and his two beasts, this is something I have not only been told from heaven but have also been shown in the world of spirits that is below heaven. I have seen people devoted to faith alone gathered into a crowd that looked like a great dragon whose tail was stretched out toward heaven; and I have seen separate individuals of this type who looked like dragons. In that world we see things like this because of the way spiritual and earthly phenomena correspond to each other. That is also why heaven's angels call these people dragons.

There are many kinds of these people, though—some who form the head of the dragon, some who form the body, and some who form the tail. The ones who form the tail are the ones who distort everything that is true in the Word, which is why in the Book of Revelation it says of the dragon that its tail drew down a third of the stars of heaven [Revelation 12:4]. "The stars of heaven" means knowledge concerning what is true, and "a third" means all.

57 Now, since in the Book of Revelation the dragon means people devoted to a faith divorced from caring, and since this has not been known before and has been hidden because the spiritual meaning of the Word has not been recognized, I need to offer at this point an overview of the meaning of what is said about the dragon in the twelfth chapter [of Revelation].

58 This is what the twelfth chapter of Revelation says about the dragon:

And a great sign appeared in heaven: a woman clothed with the sun, with the moon under her feet, and on her head a crown of twelve stars. And being pregnant, she cried out in labor and in pain to give birth. And another sign appeared in heaven: behold, a great red dragon having seven heads and ten horns, and seven gems on his heads. His tail drew a third of the stars of heaven and threw them to the earth. And the dragon stood before the woman who was about to give birth, to devour her child as soon as it was born. She bore a male child who was to rule all nations with a rod of iron. And her child was caught up to God and his throne. And the woman fled into the wilderness, where she has a place prepared by God, so that they would feed her there for one thousand two hundred and sixty days. And war broke out in heaven: Michael and his angels fought with the dragon; and the dragon and his angels fought, but they did not prevail, and no place was found for them in heaven any longer. And when the dragon saw that he had been cast to the earth, he persecuted the woman who had given birth to the male child. But the woman was given two wings of a great eagle, so that she could fly into the wilderness to her place, where she would be nourished for a time and times and half a time, away from the presence of the serpent. So the serpent spewed water out of his mouth like a flood after the woman, to cause her to be carried away by the flood. But the earth helped the woman, and the earth opened its mouth and swallowed up the flood that the dragon had spewed out of his mouth. And the dragon was enraged with the woman, and he went away to make war with the rest of her offspring, who keep the commandments of God and have the testimony of Jesus Christ. (Revelation 12:1–8, 13–17)

The meaning of these verses is as follows:

59

A great sign appeared in heaven means a revelation by the Lord concerning a church that is to be, and concerning how its teachings will be received and who will attack it.

A woman clothed with the sun, with the moon under her feet means a church that has love and faith from the Lord.

And on her head a crown of twelve stars means that the people [of that church] will have wisdom and intelligence arising from divine truths.

And being pregnant means the new teachings being born.

She cried out in labor and in pain to give birth means resistance by those people who were devoted to a faith divorced from caring.

And another sign appeared in heaven means a further revelation.

Behold, a great red dragon means a faith divorced from caring, which is called "red" because of its strictly earthly love.

Having seven heads means a distorted understanding of the Word.

And ten horns means the power they have because many people adopt [their point of view].

And seven gems on his heads means distorted truths of the Word.

His tail drew a third of the stars of heaven and threw them to the earth means the destruction of all recognition of what is true.

And the dragon stood before the woman who was about to give birth, to devour her child as soon as it was born means their hatred of and intent to destroy the teachings of the church at its very beginning.

She bore a male child means new teachings.

Who was to rule all nations with a rod of iron means teachings that will carry conviction because of the power of earthly truth derived from spiritual truth.

And her child was caught up to God and his throne means that those teachings will be kept safe by the Lord and heaven.

And the woman fled into the wilderness means the church among few people.

Where she has a place prepared by God means that its state is such that in the meantime it may be made available to many.

So that they would feed her there for one thousand two hundred and sixty days means until it grows to its appointed size.

And war broke out in heaven: Michael and his angels fought with the dragon, and the dragon and his angels fought means the disagreement and battle of those devoted to a faith divorced from caring against those devoted to the teachings of the church with respect to the Lord and a life of caring.

But they did not prevail means that [those devoted to faith alone] yielded.

And no place was found for them in heaven any longer means their being cast down.

And when the dragon saw that he had been cast to the earth, he persecuted the woman who had given birth to the male child means an attack on the church on account of its teachings by those devoted to a faith divorced from caring.

But the woman was given two wings of a great eagle, so that she could fly into the wilderness to her place means caution while it was still among few.

Where she would be nourished for a time and times and half a time, away from the presence of the serpent means until the church would grow to its appointed size.

So the serpent spewed water out of his mouth like a flood after the woman, to cause her to be carried away by the flood means their rationalizations based on abundant distortions aimed at the destruction of the church.

But the earth helped the woman, and the earth opened its mouth and swallowed up the flood that the dragon had spewed out of his mouth means that because the rationalizations were based on distortions, they collapsed on their own.

And the dragon was enraged with the woman, and he went away to make war with the rest of her offspring means their abiding hatred.

Who keep the commandments of God and have the testimony of Jesus Christ means against those who live caring lives and believe in the Lord.

60   In the next chapter of Revelation, chapter 13, the subject is the dragon's two beasts, the one that was seen rising up out of the sea and the one that was seen rising up out of the earth. Verses 1–10 are about the first and verses 11–18 about the second. We can see from verses 2, 4, and 11 that these are the dragon's beasts. The first beast means faith divorced from caring with respect to the confirmations it draws from the earthly self, and the second means faith divorced from caring with respect to the confirmations it draws from the Word, which are in fact distortions of the truth. I will forgo an explanation of all this, though, since these verses reflect the lines of reasoning [of those devoted to faith divorced from caring], and require a great deal of verbiage to expound. [I will limit myself to] the last one: "Let those who understand calculate the number of the beast. It is the number of a human being; its number is six hundred and sixty-six" (Revelation 13:18). "Let those who understand calculate the number of the beast" means that those who are enlightened should examine the nature of the confirmations of that faith that have been drawn from the Word. "It is the number of a human being" means that those confirmations are of the same nature as the self-centered understandings [of those who hold that faith]; and "its number is six hundred and sixty-six" means that it is a distortion of everything true in the Word.

The Goats Mentioned in Daniel and Matthew Symbolize People Devoted to a Faith Divorced from Caring

WE can tell that the goat in the eighth chapter of Daniel and the goats in the twenty-fifth chapter of Matthew mean people devoted to a faith divorced from caring, because in those passages they are set in contrast to a ram and sheep, and rams and sheep mean people who are devoted to caring. In the Word the Lord is called the Shepherd, the church is called the fold, the people of the church in general are called the flock, and the individuals are called sheep; and since sheep mean people devoted to caring, in these passages goats mean people who are not devoted to caring.

62   Reference to the following is needed to show that goats mean people who are devoted to a faith divorced from caring:

1. Experience in the spiritual world
2. Those on whom the Last Judgment was carried out
3. The description of the battle between the ram and the goat in Daniel
4. Lastly, the failure of caring in the people described in Matthew

63   1. *Experience in the spiritual world shows that in the Word, goats mean people who are devoted to a faith divorced from caring.* In the spiritual world we can see everything we see in this earthly world. We can see houses and mansions, parks and gardens with all kinds of trees in them. We can see fields and farmland, plains and meadows, as well as herds and flocks, all looking much as they do in our world. In fact, the only difference is that those in our world come from an earthly origin, while those in the spiritual world come from a spiritual origin. Since angels are spiritual, they see things that are from a spiritual origin just the way we see things that are from an earthly origin.

[2] Everything visible in the spiritual world is a correspondence. That is, everything corresponds to something the angels and spirits are feeling. That is why people who are moved by what is good and true and who therefore enjoy wisdom and intelligence live in splendid mansions that are surrounded by gardens with an abundance of trees (all of which things are correspondences), and these in turn are surrounded by farmlands and fields where flocks lie at rest (all of which things are manifestations).

For people who are drawn to evil, the correspondences are quite the opposite. These people are either confined to windowless workhouses in the hells where the only light is like that of marsh gas, or live in shacks in the wilderness where everything around is barren, where there are snakes, lizards, owls, and many other things that correspond to their evils.

[3] There is an intermediate space between heaven and hell called the world of spirits. That is where we all arrive immediately after death. We interact with each other there much the way we do here on earth; and there as well, everything we see is a correspondence. We see gardens and groves there, forests with trees and bushes, and green, flowery meadows, along with all kinds of animals, tame and wild, all corresponding to what we are feeling.

[4] I have often seen sheep and goats there and fights between them like the one described in the eighth chapter of Daniel [Daniel 8:2–14]. I have seen goats with horns bent forward or backward and have seen them

angrily attacking sheep. I once saw goats with two horns using them to batter some sheep, and when I looked to see what was happening, I saw some people arguing about caring and faith. I could see from this that what looked like a goat was faith divorced from caring and that what looked like a sheep was a caring that gave rise to faith.

Because I have seen this so often, I have been granted the opportunity to know for certain that in the Word, goats mean people devoted to a faith divorced from caring.

2. *Those on whom the Last Judgment was carried out show that goats in the Word mean people who are devoted to a faith divorced from caring.* The Last Judgment was carried out exclusively on people who were moral on the outside but not spiritual on the inside—or at best were only slightly spiritual within. Those who had been both outwardly and inwardly evil, though, had been consigned to hell long before the Last Judgment, and those who had been both outwardly and inwardly spiritual had been raised into heaven long before the Last Judgment. This is because the judgment was not carried out on people in heaven or people in hell but on people who were halfway between heaven and hell and were making what seemed to be heavens for themselves there.

[2] You can see in *Last Judgment* 59 and 70 that the Last Judgment was on these individuals and these only; and there is further relevant information in *Supplement on the Last Judgment* [16–22] where it discusses Protestants. These passages show that people were consigned to hell if they were devoted both in theory and in practice to a faith divorced from caring, but that they were raised into heaven if they were committed to this same faith in theory only but were nevertheless devoted to leading caring lives. I could see from this that these were just what the Lord meant by the goats and the sheep in Matthew 25:[32–33], where it speaks of the Last Judgment.

3. *The description of the battle between the ram and the goat in Daniel shows that in the Word, goats mean people who are devoted to a faith divorced from caring.* Spiritually understood, everything in Daniel, like everything in Sacred Scripture as a whole (as noted in *Sacred Scripture* 5–26), is about matters of heaven and the church. This then holds true for what it says in chapter 8 about the battle between the ram and the goat, as follows:

> In a vision I saw a ram that had two tall horns, the taller of which rose up behind [the other]. With its horn the ram pushed westward, northward, and southward and became enormous.

Then I saw a goat that came from the west across the surface of the whole earth; it had a horn between its eyes. It charged at the ram in the fury of its strength, broke the ram's two horns, and cast the ram to the ground and trampled it. The large horn of the goat was broken, and four horns sprang up in its place. A little horn came out of one of them, which grew tremendously toward the south, toward the dawn, and toward the glory, and even to the host of the heavens, and cast down to earth some of the host and some of the stars, and trampled them. The goat even exalted itself toward the Leader of the Host, and took the daily offerings away from him and cast down the dwelling place of his sanctuary, because it cast truth to the ground. And I heard a holy one saying, "How long will this vision last concerning the daily offerings and this destructive sinning, the trampling of the holy place and the host?" And he said, "Until the evening [and] the morning: then the holy place will be set right." (Daniel 8:2–14)

66 It is obvious that this vision is predicting future states of the church, since it says that the goat took the daily offerings away from the Leader of the Host, that it cast down the dwelling place of his sanctuary, and that it cast truth to the ground. It also says that a holy one said, "How long will this vision last concerning the daily offerings and this destructive sinning, the trampling of the holy place and the host?" and that this would continue until the evening and the morning: then the holy place will be set right. Evening serves to mean the end of a church when there must be a new one.

The kings of Media and Persia later in this chapter [Daniel 8:20] mean much the same as the ram, and the king of Greece means much the same as the goat, because in the Word the names of realms, nations, and peoples, as well as those of persons and places, mean matters of heaven and the church.

67 The interpretation is as follows:

The ram that had two tall horns, the taller of which rose up behind [the other], means people devoted to a faith prompted by caring.

With its horn the ram pushed westward, northward, and southward means the scattering of what is evil and false.

Its becoming enormous means growth.

The goat that came from the west across the surface of the whole earth means people devoted to a faith divorced from caring and their invasion of the church (the west is the evil of the earthly self).

Its having a horn between its eyes means intellectual pride.

Its charging at the ram in the fury of its strength means a violent attack against caring and its faith.

Its breaking the ram's two horns and casting the ram to the ground and trampling it means its complete scattering of both caring and faith, since scattering either one is scattering the other—they make a single entity.

The large horn of the goat being broken means the end of the illusion of intellectual pride.

The four horns springing up in its place means using the literal meaning of the Word for support.

A little horn coming out of one of them means the claim that no one can fulfill the law or do any good on his or her own.

Its growing tremendously toward the south, toward the dawn, and toward the glory means a consequent rebelliousness throughout the whole church.

Doing this even to the host of the heavens, and casting down some of the host and some of the stars and trampling them means in this way destroying all awareness of what is good and true, the very substance of caring and faith.

Even exalting itself toward the Leader of the Host, taking the daily offerings away from him and casting down the dwelling place of his sanctuary means that this entailed the ravaging of every aspect of the worship of the Lord and every aspect of his church.

Casting truth to the ground means the distortion of the truth of the Word.

Until the evening [and] the morning: then the holy place will be set right means the end of that church and the beginning of a new one.

4. *The failure of caring in the people described in Matthew shows that goats mean people who are devoted to a faith divorced from caring.* We can see that the goats and sheep in Matthew 25:31–46 have the same meaning as the goat and the ram in Daniel because deeds of caring are listed for the sheep and it says that they did them, and the same deeds of caring are listed for the goats but it says that they did not do them, and that this is why these latter are condemned. A neglect of deeds is characteristic of people who are devoted to a faith divorced from caring because of their refusal to believe that deeds have anything to do with salvation or the church. When people so set aside caring—which consists of deeds—then faith fails as well, because faith comes out of caring; and when there is neither caring nor faith, there is damnation.

If the goats in this passage had meant all evil people it would have listed all the evil things they did rather than all the deeds of caring they did not do.

People like this are also meant by goats in Zechariah:

> My wrath blazes against the shepherds, and I will execute judgment
> upon the goats. (Zechariah 10:3)

And in Ezekiel:

> Behold, I am judging between sheep and sheep, between rams and
> goats. Is it too little for you to have eaten up the good pasture? Will
> you also trample what remains of the food with your feet? You attack
> all the weak sheep with your horns until you have scattered them.
> Therefore I will save my flock, so that it will no longer be prey. (Ezekiel
> 34:17, 18, 21, 22, and following)

A Faith Divorced from Caring Destroys the Church and Everything It Stands For

69 A faith divorced from caring is no faith at all because caring is the life of faith, its soul, its essence; and where there is no faith because there is no caring, there is no church. That is why the Lord says,

> When the Son of Humanity comes, will he find faith on the earth?
> (Luke 18:8)

70 From time to time I have heard "goats" and "sheep" discussing whether people devoted to a faith divorced from caring have any truth; and since some said they have a great deal, the contested issue was put to a test. They were asked whether they knew what love is, what caring is, and what good is, and since these were things they had divorced themselves from, all they could reply was that they did not know.

They were asked what sin is, what repentance is, and what the forgiveness of sins is. They replied that people who are justified by their faith are forgiven their sins so that their sins will no longer be in evidence. They were told that this is not the truth.

They were asked what regeneration is. They replied that it is either baptism or the forgiveness of sins by means of faith. They were told that this is not the truth.

They were asked what constitutes a spiritual person. They replied that a spiritual person is someone who is "justified by the faith we profess"; but they were told that this is not the truth.

They were asked about redemption, about the union of the Father and the Lord, and about the oneness of God, and they gave answers that are not truths—and so it went.

After the questions and answers, the debate was submitted to judgment; and the decision was that people who had convinced themselves of a faith divorced from caring had no truth whatever.

In this world, we cannot believe that this is in fact the case, because when people are convinced of things that are false they cannot help but see those false things as true and find little point in knowing more than what their faith tells them. Further, their faith is divorced from their intellect. That is, it is a blind faith, so they ask no questions; and this subject can be explored only on the basis of the Word as understood through enlightenment. This means that the truths the Word contains are turned into falsities by their thinking "faith" when they see "love," "repentance," "the forgiveness of sins," and many other words that concern things that we need to do.

Make no mistake, though. That is what people are like when they convince themselves of faith alone in both theory and practice. It does not apply to people who turn their backs on evils because they are sins even though they have heard and believed that faith alone saves.

BIOGRAPHICAL NOTE

Biographical Note

EMANUEL SWEDENBORG (1688–1772) was born Emanuel Swedberg (or Svedberg) in Stockholm, Sweden, on January 29, 1688 (Julian calendar). He was the third of the nine children of Jesper Swedberg (1653–1735) and Sara Behm (1666–1696). At the age of eight he lost his mother. After the death of his only older brother ten days later, he became the oldest living son. In 1697 his father married Sara Bergia (1666–1720), who developed great affection for Emanuel and left him a significant inheritance. His father, a Lutheran clergyman, later became a celebrated and controversial bishop, whose diocese included the Swedish churches in Pennsylvania and in London, England.

After studying at the University of Uppsala (1699–1709), Emanuel journeyed to England, the Netherlands, France, and Germany (1710–1715) to study and work with leading scientists in western Europe. Upon his return he apprenticed as an engineer under the brilliant Swedish inventor Christopher Polhem (1661–1751). He gained favor with Sweden's King Charles XII (1682–1718), who gave him a salaried position as an overseer of Sweden's mining industry (1716–1747). Although Emanuel was engaged, he never married.

After the death of Charles XII, Emanuel was ennobled by Queen Ulrika Eleonora (1688–1741), and his last name was changed to Swedenborg (or Svedenborg). This change in status gave him a seat in the Swedish House of Nobles, where he remained an active participant in the Swedish government throughout his life.

A member of the Royal Swedish Academy of Sciences, he devoted himself to studies that culminated in a number of publications, most notably a comprehensive three-volume work on natural philosophy and metallurgy (1734) that brought him recognition across Europe as a scientist. After 1734 he redirected his research and publishing to a study of anatomy in search of the interface between the soul and body, making several significant discoveries in physiology.

From 1743 to 1745 he entered a transitional phase that resulted in a shift of his main focus from science to theology. Throughout the rest of his life he maintained that this shift was brought about by Jesus Christ, who appeared to him, called him to a new mission, and opened his perception to a permanent dual consciousness of this life and the life after death.

He devoted the last decades of his life to studying Scripture and publishing eighteen theological titles that draw on the Bible, reasoning, and his own spiritual experiences. These works present a Christian theology with unique perspectives on the nature of God, the spiritual world, the Bible, the human mind, and the path to salvation.

Swedenborg died in London on March 29, 1772 (Gregorian calendar), at the age of eighty-four.